Who the Hell is Melanie Klein?

Who the hell is ?

For students, teachers and curious minds, our **carefully structured jargon-free series** helps you really get to grips with brilliant intellectuals and their inherently complex theories.

Written in an **accessible and engaging** way, each book takes you through the **life and influences** of these brilliant intellectuals, before taking a deep dive into three of their **key theories in plain English.**

Smart thinking made easy!

POLITICS   PSYCHOLOGY   PHILOSOPHY   SOCIOLOGY   ART HISTORY

Who the Hell is Friedrich Nietzsche?
"...accessible and unambiguous... clarity and accuracy... highly recommend this book"

Who the Hell is B.F. Skinner?
"...an outstanding biography of the man and his theories ...a must read"

Who the Hell is Karl Marx?
"...accessible without losing any depth of analysis"

Who the Hell is Jean-Jacques Rousseau?
"...this is exactly what I need. Depth of analysis, yet written in an easily digestible style."

Who the Hell is Karl Marx?
"...pulls Marx right out of that 'difficult' box into an accessible summary of his life and ideas."

Who the Hell is Melanie Klein?

And what are her theories all about?

Lucy Etherington

First published in Great Britain in 2019 by
Bowden & Brazil Ltd
Felixstowe, Suffolk, UK.

British Library Cataloguing-in-Publication Data
A CIP record for this book is available from The British Library.

ISBN 978-1-9999492-3-5

To find out more about other books and authors in this series,
visit www.whothehellis.co.uk

Contents

Introduction 1

1. Klein's Life Story 5

2. Influences on Klein's Thinking 23

3. Splitting 45

4. Projective Identification 61

5. The Depressive Position 75

6. Case Study of a Young Boy 87

Conclusion: Kleinians Today 107

Bibliography 113

Introduction

Melanie Klein is an oft-maligned yet incredibly important figure in the field of psychoanalysis. A woman, divorcee, single mother, a Hungarian-Polish Jew who lived through two World Wars in Vienna, Budapest and finally London, where she died in 1960. Her life was as dramatic and controversial as her work. A psychoanalyst of children with no medical qualifications, she dared to contradict Freud (although her intention had been to develop rather than deviate from his theories). Her work, which was based on subjective observation rather than scientific objectivity, stated that babies aren't as sweet and innocent as we think, and placed the mother, as opposed to the Freudian father, at the centre of the infant's early development – a radical act a century ago, albeit now an accepted norm. Today one wonders whether she wouldn't be celebrated as a strong, independent and self-made woman, although there is no denying she was a controversial, difficult and some would say tragic figure.

It is interesting and indeed apt that the person who created the concept of 'splitting' experienced such intense splits in her own life, most infamously with Anna Freud and the Viennese group, but also with her own children, husband and mother. As we shall see, Klein's melodramatic and bohemian early life, filled with abandonment, loss, mental illness, tragedy and conflict, will have impacted her theories. It may also explain her powerful drive to make sense of people and their relationships, with themselves and others, and her courage in facing the dark impulses that lurk in our minds, that were very much alive in Europe at that time.

The consistent reaction to Klein's theories, even now, seems to be appalled shock, partly due to the aggressive, almost Gothic language she uses to describe an infant's internal processes – Spitting, The Paranoid-Schizoid and Depressive Positions, Introjection, Projection, and the 'Good' and 'Bad' Breast. In Kleinian language, 'objects' became a term used to refer to people, which was also a ground-breaking idea that would become central to the later field of Object Relations theory.

However, the biggest objection to Klein is often around the treatment of her own children, who she abandoned in their early years due to depression (possibly post-natal) and then later psychoanalyzed (as Freud had also done to his children). Klein's daughter Melitta hated her so much that she led a campaign to have her removed from the British Psychoanalytical Society, accused her of causing her son's suicide (Klein's son Hans, who appeared to be fond of his mother, fell in a climbing accident) and refused to go to her funeral.

And yet Klein's contribution to the field of psychoanalysis, and especially child psychoanalysis, has been seminal. Without her courageously creative and eccentric way of working, we would not have the theory of Projective Identification, in which one person's unwanted feelings are projected into another. This led to a breakthrough in the understanding of counter-transference in the client–patient relationship, as analysts came to realize that clients could and often did project their feelings into the analyst. It was Klein who developed the idea of using play to explore a child's inner world using toys to represent 'objects', much as Freud would employ free association with adults. Her interpretation of the inner lives of children formed the basis of Object Relations theory, and led to the formation of the Object Relations School, which continued through Fairbairn, Winnicott, Balint, Guntrip and Bowlby, bridging the gap between Freudianism and later humanistic theories.

It's worth noting that most of her child patients, now adults, remember Klein with extreme fondness. Later in life, it seemed she softened, was open to revising her earlier theories and focused more on the vital role of love and the power of reparation in an infant's early life. We hope, in this book, to redress the balance of the way in which this extraordinary woman is seen and to respond to Klein as she did to the dark phantasies of her young patients – with honesty, acceptance and understanding.

1. Klein's Life Story

Melanie Klein was born Melanie Reizes in Vienna, Austria, on 30 March 1882. She was the youngest of four children in an intellectual and melodramatic Jewish family. Her father Moriz was a local doctor in the small Hungarian town Deutschkreutz, now part of Austria. Born to an Orthodox Jewish family, Moriz's first wife was a woman he had never seen until the day of their wedding. The marriage was, according to Klein, 'dissolved' when he was 37, although no reason is given. In his mid-40s, he met and married 25-year-old Slovakian beauty Libussa Deutsche. Witty, smart and passionate about learning, Libussa educated herself through reading and listening to her husband, in much the same way Klein would later teach herself psychoanalysis through her various father figures. In her autobiography (held by the Melanie Klein Trust), Klein remains baffled by her parents' marriage, seeing in her mother a lack of sexual passion, even revulsion for her aloof and deeply intellectual father.

They had four children – Emilie (the father's favourite) was born in 1876; Emanuel in 1877; Sidonie in 1878 (dying just eight years later of tuberculosis); and finally Melanie, who came along in 1882. Between the births of Sidonie and Melanie, the family decamped

Fig. 1 Melanie Klein, aged 7–8, c.1890

to a squalid part of Vienna in the mistaken belief they would be better off there.

While both came from Orthodox families, Moriz and Libussa adhered to Jewish ceremonies more from a sense of tradition than true piety. At one point, Libussa tried to create a kosher household, but was defeated by her strong-willed children. Moriz, no doubt through the anti-Semitism rampant at the time, was only able to find employment as a dental assistant, while also working part-time as a medical assistant to a vaudeville theatre. Libussa, to her shame and chagrin, was forced to support the family financially by opening a shop, which rather eccentrically sold reptiles and plants.

Melanie would have a difficult relationship with her mother throughout her life – she claims in her autobiographical notes that she was the only one of the four children not to have been breast-fed. She was also told that she was a 'mistake', but despite this slightly hostile beginning she was determined to shine. The competition and enmeshment between siblings and parents in the household no doubt contributed to Klein's theories on childhood aggression and sibling envy, as well as her fascination with the ways we connect to other people (ultimately leading to her re-writing of Freud's Drive Theory as Object Relations Theory). Her role in the family was of the protégé, the precocious child genius, and she was treated by her elder sister and brother as a kind of performing intellectual pet while also being teased relentlessly. Sidonie always defended Melanie who, although only four at the time of her sister's death, wrote later that had Sidonie lived, she would have been her greatest friend. In her notes she adds that 'I have a feeling that I never entirely got over the feeling of grief for her death'.

The family's financial fortunes changed once again when Melanie was five. Her father inherited a sweepstake ticket along with his father's savings when he died, and the ticket won 10,000 forints (then worth around $10,000 US, according to the official exchange rate at the time). Newly wealthy, Moriz bought a dental practice and the family moved into a large apartment in middle-class Martinstrasse in Währing, then a suburb of Vienna. In this period of affluence, Melanie had nannies or what she rather grandly called her 'French governesses'. When she was eight or nine, she was 'tortured' by the belief that she would turn Catholic, the predominant religion in Vienna at the time. As a Jewish child, she would have been aware of her outsider status as a member of a persecuted minority: and indeed, psychoanalysis became for many Jews a form of religion, demanding utter devotion.

Melanie did exceptionally well at school and entered the Vienna gymnasium aged 16, hoping to become a doctor. It is said that she longed for her father's approval, but he remained distant; he was in his 50s when she was born and died in 1900, when she was only 18 years old and long before he could see her ambition realized. His lack of interest in her had a profound effect, and it hurt her deeply that he often openly expressed his preference for her more subdued older sister, Emilie. This lack of fatherly love adds a poignant layer to Melanie's later desperate need for Freud's approval and perhaps explains her hurt at his aloofness and rejection, especially when she felt that her theories grew from his own. Her father's preference for Emilie also echoes in Klein's infamous rivalry with Freud's daughter, Anna.

Fin de Siècle Vienna

Vienna, the city Freud and Klein shared for over a decade at the turn of the 20th century, was a hotbed of creative, political and intellectual thought, a clash of old and new. As the Habsburg Empire (Austria and Hungary) and its values began to fragment, new demands for human rights emerged. Between 1870 and 1910 the population of Vienna and Budapest tripled. A collection of artists, architects, musicians, social scientists and politicians would transform their individual fields and come to define the modern world as we know it.

Prominent figures in the city included Adolf Loos (pioneer of modern architecture and friend of the philosopher Ludwig Wittgenstein), composer Arnold Schönberg, and writers Peter Altenberg and Karl Kraus. The artist Gustav Klimt introduced the Viennese to modernism and helped launch the careers of artists Oskar Kokoschka and Egon Shiele. The city's mayor Karl Lueger, was famously anti-Semitic, declaring 'I will decide who is a Jew'. In 1908, failing artist Adolf Hitler moved to Vienna and became an admirer of Lueger, later praising his popular appeal in his manifesto, *Mein Kampf* (1925).

The first wave of feminism was sweeping across Europe in the mid-19th and early 20th centuries. In the Austro-Hungarian Empire capitals of Vienna and Budapest, groups were springing up to fight for women's rights, and in 1908, Else Jerusalem wrote a book entitled *The Red House*, detailing the treatment of Vienna's 50,000 prostitutes. In a city and time where sex was not spoken about and prostitutes were not acknowledged, the book effectively blew the lid off polite society.

Libussa, Emanuel and Melanie were a tight-knit, manipulative and melodramatic unit, distinct from the pairing of the quieter father and elder daughter. Melanie was the pet project of her adored and feckless brother who, inspired by Nietzsche, was determined to write and live at a level of intense passion and creativity and he encouraged Melanie to do the same. He taught her Greek and Latin and she would write poems and plays inspired by the playwright Arthur Schnitzler.

In this period, Emanuel, seriously ill with TB, travelled to Europe to pursue a warmer climate and the lifestyle of the romantic artist, adding to the family's financial troubles in the process. In 1900, Moriz passed away without much ceremony, apparently of pneumonia. Emanuel, who had a fractious relationship with his father, did not learn about his death for two months. Emanuel's letters home are emotionally heightened and self-pitying and describe his hypomanic self-destruction from alcohol, drugs, poverty (which he blamed on his mother, who sent him 'a pittance' to live on, rather than on his gambling debts) and doomed relationships. They also describe an incestuous possessiveness, for both his sister and mother.

Photographs of this time show young Melanie as a voluptuous beauty and, with her intellectual talents, her brother Emmanuel liked to show her off to his friends, many of whom fell in love with her. One of those friends was Arthur Klein (1876–1939) a

Fig. 2 Melanie Klein, aged 17, 1899

studious chemical engineer and second cousin on her mother's side. She was attracted to his intellectual gifts rather than his looks and it also helped that Emanuel was initially impressed by him. On learning of the engagement, however, Emanuel became jealous. Libussa, in turn, seems to have been envious of the infatuation between brother and sister, and she endeavoured to keep them apart when he briefly returned home. As Melanie's marriage approached, Emanuel told her that she was the reason he had holes in his shoes and was starving, as all their mother's money was being spent on her. He began to make regular references to his death, and also to Arthur's 'masculinity', suggesting Melanie's fiancé would not remain faithful to her. Emanuel's sadistic cruelty to his sister could have been exaggerated by cocaine, widely used in the 1880s as a cure for pain, as well as his morphine addiction. His letters ceased in October 1902, except for a brief, bitter note to Melanie that he wrote in Genoa, a few hours before his death on 1 December. He had suffered heart failure at the young age of just 25. As he probably intended, Melanie carried the guilt of his death for the rest of her life.

While still in a state of mourning, Melanie finally married Arthur on 31 March 1903, the day after her 21st birthday. They moved to Rosenberg and within two months, Melanie discovered she was pregnant. She gave birth to Melitta on 19 January 1904. She records in her autobiography that she felt unhappy and trapped but was determined to throw herself into motherhood. She breast-fed Melitta for seven months, but when Melitta was a year old, Melanie left her in the charge of the all-powerful Libussa while she went travelling with Arthur. It was around this time that Melanie became depressed, although Libussa would describe it as 'nerves'. Melanie's depression became more marked after she published a book of her brother's writing in 1906. It was also at this time that she became pregnant with her second child, Hans, who was born on 2 March, 1907.

Libussa moved in to 'help' and took command of the household while Melanie was encouraged to travel, which was always seen by the family as a great antidote to depression. Letters from Libussa passive-aggressively reiterate who is the better mother, no doubt adding to Melanie's guilt and anxiety about leaving her children. She clearly wanted Melanie out of the way, and contrived to keep husband and wife apart, too. It seems she wanted to keep Melanie in a perpetual state of childlike dependency, doing everything she could to prevent her growing up. In 1909, filled with despair, Melanie took herself to a sanatorium in Chur, Switzerland for two and a half months. When Melanie returned, she battled with her mother for dominance of the household, leading to Libussa's breakdown: she was sent to Karlsbad for the 'cure' and, naturally, Melanie felt entirely responsible.

Budapest and the Outbreak of WWI

In 1910, the Kleins (plus Libussa) moved to Budapest, 'with theatres, parties and pleasant company' according to Melanie's autobiographical notes, but where anti-Semitism was rife. Arthur's relatives, who Melanie liked, lived there, and his sister Jolan became her very close friend. While proudly if not religiously Jewish, Melanie had her children baptized in the Unitarian Church, no doubt in a protective move. She continued to struggle with her 'nerves', which may have been exacerbated by the presence of her mother.

Although the outbreak of war had relatively little impact on the Hungarian capital, Melanie's husband, Arthur, was called up. This was a traumatizing experience that impacted the marriage. On 1 July 1914, Melanie gave birth to her third child, Erich, after which the health of Libussa rapidly deteriorated. Diagnosed with bronchitis on November 6th of the same year, Libussa died. Melanie was distraught and wracked with guilt that she should have done more.

While male psychoanalysts were enriching their understanding of trauma with shell-shocked soldiers during and after the First World War, Melanie was suffering the breakdown of her marriage, depression, and bereavement following the death of her mother. This led her to seek help, first at various Swiss clinics, then with 'the best nerve specialist' in Budapest, Sándor Ferenczi.

Ferenczi (1873–1933) was one of Freud's closest associates, and it was around this time that Melanie read Freud's 1901 paper 'On Dreams', which sparked her interest in the practice. Ferenczi, while analyzing Melanie, discovered that she had a 'gift' for understanding children and encouraged her to begin her own analytical practice. And so began her life-long love of psychoanalysis. Having joined the Hungarian Psychoanalytic Society, and on the verge of her ascendency, Hungary fell to a

Communist regime and Jews were barred from professions and universities. Arthur took a job in Sweden, while Melanie and her children went to her in-laws in Slovakia.

Berlin 1921–1926

Unable to return to Hungary, Melanie and the children moved to Berlin in 1921, the beginning of the Golden Twenties, the Weimar Republic era and its heyday as a major world city. Einstein was awarded the Nobel Prize for Physics in 1921 and lived there until the Nazis rose to power. Expressionism was still the popular art form, Bauhaus the architectural, and cinema was huge. It was considered highly decadent and subversive; the Nazis called it 'the reddest city in Europe after Moscow'.

Klein and Arthur were by now separated, and he apparently formed another attachment in Sweden. The couple briefly made an attempt at a reconciliation, playing 'happy families' in a new home. But there were ugly quarrels, with Arthur bullying Hans and trying to get custody of Erich. Melitta, meanwhile, had entered Berlin University to study medicine and began training as an analyst, marrying a well-connected Viennese aristocrat, Walter Schmideberg in 1924. Melanie and Arthur finally divorced in 1926.

Around this time, Klein entered analysis with Karl Abraham (1877–1925) for two years before his sudden death in 1925. Like Ferenczi, Abraham was a mentor as well as her therapist, giving her support in what was an unpleasant environment for her. He had been involved in setting up the first psychoanalytic *Poliklinik* in Berlin in 1920 (see Chapter 2), which was packed with psychoanalytic pioneers lured from Vienna and Budapest, but also British students such as Edward Glover (1888–1972). Melanie's brilliance here in clinical observation, creativity and intellectual rigour impressed her peers, including the American-born British psychoanalyst, Alix Strachey (1887–1967), who was in Berlin for analysis with Abraham. She admired Klein's intelligence, the way she went about grappling with her theories, and her fearlessness in disagreeing with others in her field, such as dismissing fellow female analyst Hermine Hug-Hellmuth (1871–1924) as 'sentimental'.

Dancing Partners

By the end of 1924, Melanie and Alix Strachey had become unlikely friends – one tall, angular and boyish, the other short, Jewish and eccentric. Alix was a member of the bohemian intellectual set known as the Bloomsbury group, as was her husband, James Strachey, and his younger brother, the author Lytton Strachey. The Stracheys went to Vienna to be analyzed by Freud in the 1920s and were entrusted with translating his works, some of which were printed by the Hogarth Press, the publishing company run by Virginia and Leonard Woolf. They would also translate Klein's work, no doubt enhancing her popularity in Britain with the Bloomsbury style. Despite a lack of qualification, other than a Bachelor of Arts from prestigious schools, both the Stracheys became practising analysts and members of the British Society, for which they received Freud's blessing.

Alix introduced Melanie to neurologist and psychoanalyst Ernest Jones (1879–1958) and other members of the British Psychoanalytical Society, and as a result Klein was invited to London for the first time in 1925 to deliver a series of lectures.

Alix was supposed to be teaching Melanie English, but the two women spent most of their time in post-war Berlin going to parties and balls. Alix wrote to her husband of Melanie 'most elaborately got up as a kind of Cleopatra – terribly *décolleté* – and covered in bangles and rouge'.

In 1925, when she was supposedly consumed with the preparation for her London lectures, Melanie started attending a dancing class and became romantically involved with her dancing partner Chezkel Zvi Kloetzel. Kloetzel was a journalist on the *Berliner Tageblatt*, nine years younger than Klein and with a daughter. He was also a well-known ladies man. Not only did he bear a striking similarity to Emanuel, Klein's secret nickname for him was Hans, the name of her older son (a fact that would not be considered insignificant by a psychoanalyst).

London, England and The Bloomsbury Set

Klein arrived in England in July 1925 (while still with Kloetzel) to deliver her lectures to the British Psychoanalytical Society. She was incredibly nervous about delivering her theories in English and had trouble finding the right words. But at last, she had found an appreciative audience. The locale was 50 Gordon Square, the drawing room of Karin and Adrian Stephen (Virginia Woolf's brother), right in the heart of Bloomsbury. Those attending included psychoanalysts Ernest Glover, Sylvia Payne (1880–1976), John Rickman (1891–1951), Joan Riviere (1883–1962), Ella Sharpe (1875–1947) and Susan Isaacs (1885–1948), who was later to become Klein's closest colleague. Melanie describes the lectures in her autobiographical notes as 'one of the happiest times of my life. I found such friendliness, hospitality and interest'.

Melanie Klein was exactly the sort of person the Bloomsbury set was drawn to: intelligent, controversial and openly challenging of male-dominated views. Virginia Woolf later described Klein in her 1939 diary as 'a woman of character and force and some submerged – how shall I say – not craft but subtlety: something working underground. A pull, a twist, like an undertow: menacing. A bluff, grey-haired lady with large, imaginative eyes'.

Those three weeks concreted her decision to move to England: at last she had found a home for her ideas. The following year she moved to London. She was invited by Ernest Jones, lifelong friend and biographer of Freud, to analyze his children and later his wife. She was joined by her son Erich three months later, while her other children continued their education in Berlin. After renting a few flats, she found 63 Linden Gardens in Notting Hill, which became her home and consulting rooms.

Divisions and Loss

At the same time that Klein was experiencing a breakthrough in her career, she also suffered a blow when Karl Abraham, her mentor and analyst, fell ill and finally died on Christmas day in 1925. In her private papers, Klein describes the sudden end of her analysis with Abraham and his death as a very painful time (Melanie Klein Trust).

In August 1927, Melitta graduated with distinction from the Berlin University, then followed her mother to London in 1928, moving into Linden Gardens where the waiting room was made into a bedroom for her. Her brother Erich also lived in the household. By 1930 Melitta was regularly attending meetings of the British Society, where she read papers that seemed to support her mother's views. At first things seem to have been amicable between mother and daughter, but then Melitta – who had begun psychoanalysis under Karen Horney in Berlin – entered analysis with Edward Glover, and things began to change. In a letter to her mother, clearly dis-entangling herself from what she considered to be a neurotically co-dependent relationship with a narcissistic parent, Melitta wrote:

> 'You have a strong tendency towards trying to enforce your way of viewing, of feeling, your interests, your friends, etc, onto me. I am now a grown up, and must be independent...don't forget that through our shared profession a difficult situation is created: this could most certainly be solved if you treated me like another colleague and allowed me all the freedom of thinking and expression of opinion, as you do the others.' (Melitta Schmideberg, letter to Melanie Klein, August 1934)

By late 1933, Melitta and Glover had joined forces in what appeared to be a vicious campaign to discredit Melanie Klein, with Society meetings often interrupted by Melitta's heckling of her mother. Reasons for their bitterness are not entirely clear, although Klein's abrasive manner and theories had alienated many Society members. It has been suggested that Melitta was deeply disturbed with a father-complex (not unlike her mother) and Glover exploited this. There are also speculations that things emerged during analysis, or perhaps transference and counter-transference were at play.

At this time, Klein moved to a larger house at 42 Clifton Hill, St John's Wood, London. She invited Freud's architect son Ernst

– who had also designed the *Poliklinik* in Berlin – to design the interior, as his first commission in England. The style was classic Bauhaus, which was daring for a Regency house. (Later, sculptor Oscar Nemon produced a twice life-size bust of her for the garden – he had already made busts of Freud and Jones. Klein loathed it and hid it in the attic for years before destroying it).

In 1934, Melanie's son Hans died when walking in the Tatra Mountains, which border Slovakia and Poland, plunging to his death from a crumbling precipice. His funeral was in Budapest, but Melanie was too distraught to leave London. Melitta's reaction was that her brother had not fallen but deliberately taken his own life, and she pointed the finger of blame squarely at their mother. It seems many members of the British Society were also prepared to take this view, and from this time onward, Klein and her work came under almost constant attack.

The War Years, Cambridge and Scotland

In late August 1939, Klein went on holiday to Walberswick in Suffolk, England, at the same time learning that her ex-husband Arthur had died in Sion, Switzerland. On September 3rd, 1939, Britain declared war on Germany and the day Germany invaded Poland, Klein went to Bishop's Stortford, north of London, and moved in with her friend and colleague Susan Isaacs. On the 23rd, Sigmund Freud died, and Klein moved for the duration of the war to Cambridge. With Erich expecting to be called up, Klein tried to persuade her daughter-in-law Judy and grandson Michael to join her, but Judy – who often felt her mother-in-law to be controlling and intrusive – resisted and stayed in London.

Klein's sister Emilie died in 1940 and Klein again felt guilty at not being there. It seems she tried to work through her grief by revising her paper on 'Mourning and its Relation to Manic Depressive States', which was very much inspired by the work of Freud and Abraham, but took it further. Her paper focused on how loss reactivates the early childhood psychodrama of internal objects and includes a 'phase of triumph'– the feeling the mourner has triumphed by being alive, arousing guilt and ambivalent feelings towards the dead person. Klein's most powerful work seems to be that which mines her own deepest emotional states and experiences.

Around this time Klein started seeing a young patient and when he moved with his parents to Pitlochry in the mountains of Scotland, she went with them, continuing his analysis. The boy became the subject of her monumental case study, 'Narrative of a Child Analysis' (see Chapter 6: Case Study of a Young Boy).

Final Years

In 1944, Glover retired, Melitta went to America, and Klein was left to develop and consolidate some of her most important theories, such as Splitting and Projective Identification (see Chapters 3 and 4), finding new ways to make them more comprehensive and applicable to adults with more serious psychiatric disorders. She worked on her autobiography, where she spoke of her fondness for her three grandchildren, especially her son Erich's child Michael. She analyzed Donald Winnicott's wife Clare (a fractious experience) and established a Kleinian school, although she famously said she could never be a Kleinian herself. She also famously commented: 'I am a Freudian, but not an Anna Freudian'.

Her didactic, eccentric character continued to annoy – particularly the infamous existentialist psychoanalyst R.D. Laing (1927–89), one of her supervisees, who nevertheless admired her theories, intellect and bravery in exploring the darker recesses of the psyche – while her students were inspired. She went to the theatre and concerts with friends, wrote a poignant paper 'On the Sense of Loneliness', which she delivered to the Copenhagen Congress in 1959 (published in 1963). But beneath the make-up, bright lipstick and occasional sparkle, her health was clearly deteriorating.

In 1960, Klein collapsed while on holiday and was brought home by her devoted colleague Esther Bick (1901–83). She was diagnosed with cancer of the colon. Even in hospital, after her operation, she was reportedly intent on exploring the experience of death. She spoke frankly of her funeral, saying it must be non-religious. After banning her bossy night nurse from her room,

Fig. 3 Melanie Klein with her grand-daughter Diana, c.1945.

she fell out of bed and broke her hip. Complications developed, and Klein died on 22 September 1960. Her cremation in Golders Green, London, was attended by a large group of tearful analysts, but her daughter Melitta stayed away, giving a lecture in London while wearing flamboyant red boots. Erich wrote to his sister in an attempt at family reconciliation but was rebuffed.

Despite the virulence of her detractors and lack of close friends, Melanie Klein left a devoted group of students, colleagues and analysands as well as a legacy of brilliant and enduring theories. There are Kleinian analysts in many countries, all over the world, and her ideas continue to influence psychoanalytical approaches and thinking.

Melanie Klein's Timeline

Melanie Klein	World Events
1882 Melanie Reizes is born	
	1887 Charcot and Janet make the link between hysteria and split-off personalities
	1889 Freud publishes *The Interpretation of Dreams*
1903 Marries Arthur Klein; gives birth to Melitta 1904, Hans 1907, Erich 1914	
	1910 Ferenczi and Freud form the International Psychoanalytical Association
	1913 Hug-Hellmuth publishes her paper 'The Mental Life of a Child'
1914 Budapest: reads Freud's *On Dreams*; enters analysis with Sandor Ferenczi; mother dies.	**1914** Outbreak of World War I
1917 Begins practising as a child analyst	
1919 Presents first paper, a case study of her child Hans disguised as 'Fritz'	
1921 Berlin: enters analysis with Karl Abraham	**1920** Freud publishes *Beyond the Pleasure Principal*
1923 Publishes *Development of a Child*	**1923** Freud publishes *The Ego and the ID*
1925 Moves to London	
	1927 Anna Freud publishes *Introduction to the Techniques of Child Analysis*
1932 Publishes *The Psychoanalysis of Children*	
	1933 Hitler becomes world chancellor
1934 Hans dies in the Alps	
1935 Publishes 'A Contribution to the Psychogenesis of Manic-Depressive States'	
	1938 Freuds escape to London
1940 Spends the war in Pitlochry, Scotland analyzing 'Richard', the subject of her final book *Narrative of a Child Analysis*	**1939** World War II begins; Freud dies
	1940 -41 The Blitz
1942 Extraordinary Meetings and Controversial Discussions	
	1945 World War II ends
1960 Melanie Klein dies	

2. Influences on Klein's Thinking

Before psychoanalysis, mental health was treated either in Swiss sanitoriums or in asylums. Melanie Klein and her mother would sometimes go away for months to take the 'Swiss Cure', which involved mountain air, water therapy and the removal of stress. It was in these hospitals and sanitoriums that Carl Jung (1875–1961) and Sigmund Freud (1856–1939) began working as psychiatrists and neurologists, and it was through their studies and observations that a totally new theory of mind would transform the Western world's approach to mental illness.

The Birth of Psychoanalysis

Psychoanalysis was created by Viennese neurologist Sigmund Freud at the end of the 20th century. During his work with French neurologist Jean-Martin Charcot (1825–93) in Paris, Freud became fascinated by hypnosis and how it revealed the inner workings of the mind. Back in Vienna, in collaboration with his colleague Josef Breuer (1842–1925), Freud developed a new psychological treatment in which patients talked about whatever came into their heads. Through allowing his patients to 'free associate', and talk unencumbered about their dreams and memories, he discovered a concealed part of the mind that influences our thoughts and behaviour: the unconscious. In 1899, Freud published *The Interpretation of Dreams*, which described 'the royal road to the knowledge of the unconscious activities of the mind'. Through this work, he was able to reach out to fellow practitioners across Europe, most of whom travelled to Vienna to become his pupils.

In the early days, the only women in psychoanalysis were those that came to it as patients, most famously Freud's Anna O. Female sexuality was a major focus of late 19th-century medical and psychological research, particularly hysteria (from the Greek *hysterika*, meaning 'uterus') and women's so-called sexual frigidity. Early psychoanalysis, as written by men, fixated almost entirely on repressed sexual drives from a male perspective.

The first female psychoanalyst in Europe started practising in 1913. Russian poet, novelist and philosopher, Lou Andreas-Salomé (1861–1937) was 50 years old when she met Freud at the Weimer Congress for the International Psychoanalysis Association in 1911 and she became his pupil shortly after. She was also famously the muse of German philosopher Friedrich Nietzsche (1844–1900) and the Bohemian-Austrian poet Rainer Maria Rilke (1875–1926). Andreas-Salomé became the first woman to write analytically on female sexuality and the feminine point of view, notably in *The Feminine Type* (1914). Freud was at first amused by her desire to become an analyst, but then impressed, particularly by her 1916 essay on the anal-erotic. She became close friends with the Freuds and later Anna's analyst, too.

A Male-dominated Profession

However, it was into a realm dominated by men that Melanie Klein began her psychoanalytical study of children. The initial and most important influences on her intellectual development were her analysts Sándor Ferenczi and Karl Abraham, along with the father of psychoanalysis, Sigmund Freud.

Her initial introduction into the world of psychotherapy was as a patient, entering analysis with Hungarian analyst Ferenczi in 1914 after the birth of her third child. Ferenczi became a close friend of Sigmund Freud. He is known for developing an 'active' technique, collaborating with Austrian analyst Otto Rank (1884–1939) to create 'here-and-now' psychotherapy. Ferenczi had formed The Hungarian Psychoanalytic Society in 1913, so that analysts could meet in cafés and coffee houses to discuss Freud's work. Since Freud sent every manuscript to Ferenczi before publishing it, to be a member of the Society was an enormous privilege. Ferenczi was the first analyst to see the potential in Klein, and he encouraged her to devote herself to psychoanalysis, particularly child analysis. He encouraged other female colleagues – including Anna Freud (1895–1982) – to do the same: perhaps working with children was seen as an acceptable job for a woman. Ferenczi's famous paper 'Stages in the Development of the Sense of Reality' (1913) clearly had an impact on Klein. In it he describes the omnipotent desires of a child, which he calls the 'introjection stage', and the reality stage or 'projection stage'. These ideas were to directly influence Klein's later thinking (see Chapters 4 and 5).

The International Psychoanalytical Association, started by Ferenczi and Freud in 1910, had established hubs in Vienna

(Freud), Budapest (Ferenczi), Berlin (Karl Abraham) and London (Ernest Jones). Interestingly, Klein became members of each one in turn, except Vienna, until she eventually found her intellectual home in London. Despite circling his orbit, she met Freud only once, possibly at the Berlin Congress in 1922, and was bitterly disappointed that he seemed so disinterested in her theories: she sought his approval as much as she had her father and succeeded with neither.

The Development of a Child

Ferenczi's role as psychoanalyst and professional mentor to Klein lasted for around five years. Towards the end of this period, she began to write her first psychoanalytical paper – a study of her four-year-old son, Erich, whom she was to disguise as 'Fritz'. She presented her paper to the Budapest Psychoanalytic Society in 1919, and soon afterwards was awarded membership of the Society. The paper was later published as 'The Development of a Child' (1923).

At the time that Klein was writing this paper, the White Guard – units of the new Hungarian government's National Army – were carrying out a campaign of terror, which became largely anti-Semitic as the majority of the communist revolutionaries had been Jewish. In 'The Development of a Child' there are hints that young Fritz was attacked by neighbours' children, formerly his friends, for being Jewish. Klein felt that developing in children a capacity to think for themselves – and even more importantly to question what they are told – is of vital importance. For example, Klein believed that by being made aware of his own parents' disagreement on the existence of God, Fritz could realize that those in authority do not hold absolute (objectively authoritative) views. Religious belief, she said, illustrates the pleasure principal versus the reality principal. According to Klein, all children, and some adults, would much rather give into the pleasure principal, with its superstitions and wishes, believing in their parents' omnipotence and even an omnipotent 'god' rather than face and deal with complex, disappointing and sometimes cruel reality.

Hungarian philosopher Anton Von Freund (1880–1920), who had founded The Budapest Psychoanalytic Society and recruited Klein to its membership, was unimpressed with this first version of her paper, telling Klein that she had not touched the unconscious and suggesting that she set aside a prescribed time each day to analyze the boy. She began interpreting Erich's dreams, play and fantasies in as daring a way as she would with an adult, but this seemed to have a negative effect. Erich became increasingly withdrawn and, she learned, obsessed with the contents of her stomach. He described a game he played with three toy cars, which seemed to enact the Oedipus Complex (see Chapter 5).

Ferenczi, who was also operating as a tutor to Klein, told her that he thought the sexual explanations Klein had given Erich had satisfied his curiosity, but they had also brought about an internal conflict. It was in the second version of the paper that she made one of her formative discoveries: that primal anxiety exists in children certainly at a much younger age than Freudians had formerly observed and is more oral than phallic at root.

Klein could have continued her career under the tutelage of Ferenczi and Von Freund, and it would be interesting to speculate whether they would have 'tamed' her theories; but she was forced to leave Budapest, eventually decamping to Berlin, Germany.

Abraham and The Berlin Society

At the Hague Congress in 1920, Ferenczi introduced Klein to her second mentor and later analyst, Karl Abraham, the founder of the Berlin Society of Psychoanalysis, who was also held in high regard at the British Psychoanalytical Society. Abraham was to play a big part in Klein's work and she would go on to develop his ideas, alongside the theories of Ferenczi.

Born into a Jewish family in Hamburg, Abraham trained as a psychiatrist in mental hospitals in the same group as Carl Jung. He studied the effects of psychosexual development fixation in the oral and anal stages on adult personality and psychopathology; hence the terms oral and anal fixation used to describe people who are addictive and obsessive compulsive. His theory that later mental disturbances, such as melancholic depression, began with a 'bad' mother (as opposed to Freud's rather passive Oedipal mother) clearly influenced Klein.

Both Abraham and Freud had been working for many years on the origins of depression, Freud having published 'On Mourning and Melancholia' (1917). Abraham noticed that both psychotic and neurotically depressed patients projected their own self-hatred and believed in their unconscious they had genuinely committed destructive acts. Freud called this 'omnipotence of thought', a term that Klein would later on adopt. Freud held that narcissistic identification was the basis of melancholia, and undermined Abraham's theory that depression is linked to oral-sadistic impulses. Klein, however, became more influenced by Abraham's theories on projection and introjection, described in his 1924 paper 'A Short Study of the Development of the Libido' (see Chapter 4).

As Klein learned more about the symbolic inner workings of a child's world, she also took on adult clients, and was able to see how infantile phantasies and anxieties played out in the adult psyche. Abraham taught her to write up her case histories, and Klein began writing papers on these, delivering them to the Berlin Society, of which she was made an associate member in 1922, and a full member in 1923.

Other important members of the Berlin Society included Helene Deutsch (1884–1982), one of only seven women who entered medical school at the University of Vienna in 1907. She considered herself a leader in female emancipation and became interested in female sexuality. At the same time, she focused on the role of motherhood, a theme also explored by Klein, Rank and Ferenczi. In 1944 she published *The Psychology of Women*, adding insights about female sexuality while remaining within the Freudian system. Like Freud, she believed the Oedipus Complex in girls developed from the Castration Complex.

German psychoanalyst Karen Horney (1885–1952) was also a member of the Berlin Society when Klein was there. She challenged Freud's theories, particularly around female sexuality and the instinctual drives that lay at the heart of Freudian theory. She is credited with forming a feminist psychology in response to penis envy, and coined the term 'womb envy', stating that men are driven to become successful by their inability to bear children. She disagreed with Freud that differences between men and women were inherent, arguing they were culturally and socially created. Based on her experience with her patients, she also believed neurosis was not a response to a traumatic event but evolved from early childhood experiences.

The most obvious influence on Klein's work at the time was Hermine Hug-Hellmuth (1871–1924). A Viennese schoolteacher and one of the first analysts to challenge Freud's views on women's psychology, Hug-Hellmuth's 1913 paper, 'The Mental Life of the Child: A Psychoanalytical Study' suggested a number of clinical factors in working with children that would later become obvious in Klein's work. She stressed the close observation of child patients and is credited with being the first to make use of play in a symbolic sense during analysis. While Klein was clearly influenced by Hug-Hellmuth, she ultimately dismissed the work as 'completely avoiding interpretations' (Grosskurth, 1986). Where Hug-Hellmuth felt that these should remain at an unconscious or preconscious level due to a child's fragile sense of self, Klein insisted that the child was able to bear the full weight of analytical interpretations and proceeded to discuss her own interpretations in a forthright way with them. Hug-Hellmuth's suggestion that children be treated more carefully than adults would be adopted by Klein's contemporary, Anna Freud, in direct opposition to the Kleinian approach, as shown later in this chapter.

The Symbolization of Play

Klein adopted Hug-Hellmuth's emphasis on play, giving child patients a set of toys, which she kept locked in their own personal drawers. It was during the analysis of one of her young analysands, Rita, that she first tried this method out: Rita tore up a drawing, threw the pieces in water and drank it, saying 'dead woman', which Klein recognized as the symbolic realization of anxiety.

Klein noticed that young children were capable of transference in role-play, attacking her or the toys, which she thought might have represented siblings, parents, classmates or themselves. Astute to the facial expressions of her child patients, Klein saw that when she interpreted their play, their anxiety decreased. She decided that children often have a greater capacity for insight than adults and felt strongly that her role was not to parent or educate the children, but to give the child freedom to express his or her phantasies and to interpret them.

The Influence of Freud

Sigmund Freud was perhaps the biggest influence on Klein's work – certainly in her mind he was – and she set about extending and developing his understanding of the unconscious mind. In the same way that Freud had analyzed dreams, Klein analyzed children's play, exploring the mind of the infant in a way that hadn't been done before. What she discovered was an early Oedipus complex and the very beginnings of the Superego. In her autobiographical notes (Melanie Klein Trust), she says:

> '*I kept, however, very much in mind what I thought to be the pillars of psychoanalysis discovered by Freud: the knowledge of the unconscious and its influence on the conscious; the transference situation; the importance of symbols, which Freud had elaborated in the analysis of dreams.*'

During her years in Berlin, as Klein refined her technique and developed her theories, she clearly believed that she was very much working within the Freudian tradition and seemed to be unaware, initially, of just how much her ideas diverted from his. She felt that through analyzing children at such a young age, she was able to discover vital stages of child development that her peers missed through only analyzing adults.

Klein's paper 'The Development of a Child' was published in 1923, the same year that Freud's book, *The Ego and the Id*, came out. This book had a profound effect on Klein's work. Freud's theory of personality is rooted in biological drives or instincts: Eros, the Greek god of attraction, represents the life instinct and libido; while Thanatos, who personified Death in Greek mythology, represents the death instinct, and the destructiveness within us. Freud claimed that it is in the repression of these instincts that problems arise.

Freud's theory of mind, outlined in *The Ego and The Id*, is divided into three components: the Id (primitive unconscious, a cauldron of instincts and 'primary processes' with the aim of gratification or 'pleasure principle'); the Ego (the 'I', conscious and unconscious, with the aim of self-preservation); and the Superego (a product of society and parental voices, particularly the father, with the aim of self-control).

When the Superego or Id dominate, overly repressing the instincts or letting them rule, the result is anxiety. Through analyzing 'Rita', Klein met with an extremely harsh Superego and realized that the Superego was built from the child's phantasy versions of her parents, which had become internalized (introjected). She noticed that girls' anxiety is more pronounced when it stems from a persecutory mother – whether this is a physical (external world) real mother or an internalized, imaginary one. These persecution phantasies began an internal need for reparation, which the child could gain through various forms of sublimation, and ultimately develop a healthy, well-functioning mind.

The Death Instinct

Freud's book *Beyond the Pleasure Principal* (1920) was also a huge influence on Klein's work. In it, he wrote:

> 'But how can sadistic instinct, whose aim it is to inure
> the object, be derived from Eros, the preserver of life?
> Is it not plausible to suppose that this sadism is in
> fact a death instinct, which, under the influence of the
> narcissistic libido, has been forced away from the Ego
> and has consequently emerged only in relation to the
> object?' (Freud, 1920)

Klein took this as a challenge but did not resolve it until her work in England. Unlike Freud, she interpreted the death instinct in psychological terms rather than biological. The Freudian baby is unaware of death, but the Kleinian baby experiences the death instinct at birth, as a directional pull back to the womb (and safety, oblivion), while also experiencing the life instinct as a tug in the opposite direction (but also ultimately towards death). The two drives existed symbiotically in relationship to one another. For Klein, the drives are not helpless instincts that only attach to an object almost as an afterthought, but exist in the relationship with the object. Klein began to interpret the destructive behaviour in her child patients as an expression of the death instinct, and reparation as the urge to life.

The Oedipus Complex: an Early Beginning

At the Eighth International Congress in Salzburg in April 1924, Klein presented a highly controversial paper on the technique of child analysis where she dared to place the Oedipus Complex at a much earlier stage than Freud's six to seven years. This paper would go on to become the second chapter in her book *The Psycho-Analysis of Children* (1932). Like Freud's Wolf Man, Klein's subject, Erna, had phantasies that were triggered when she witnessed her parents' copulation, even though she was only two years old at the time. Where Freud's Superego was the introjection of the parent and a good thing, Klein saw a sadistic Superego developing at the oral stage when the child's hostile feelings against its mother are turned against itself, as discussed above. Further heresy: the mother replaces the father as the castrator and seat of neuroses. By reflecting these interpretations of a child's unconscious to the child, Klein saw that children were able to differentiate between the phantasy and reality.

Hostility in Berlin

Michael Balint (1896–1970), who also escaped Budapest for Berlin and was Klein's neighbour, described her as 'already an analyst of repute who was listened to attentively, even though at times ironically. She still had an uphill fight to face, being the only non-academic and only child analyst in the midst of very "learned" German society' (Balint, 1952). He paints a picture of Klein 'courageously' using the 'naïve expressions of the nursery', which would invite 'sardonic laughter', but which went on to become an integral part of psychoanalytic knowledge.

Although Klein struggled in Berlin, faced with hostility from her fellow analysts, it was a case of right place, right time. In 1920, Max Eitingon (1881–1943) and Ernst Simmel (1882–1947), along with Karl Abraham, set up the first psychoanalytical outpatient centre, the *Poliklinik*, which was also designated as a free clinic. The Berlin Society members, including Klein, had to donate their free time to patients as part of their 'membership package'. The clinic was designed by Freud's architect son, Ernst, with the clean lines and organic structures inspired by Loos and Bauhaus. It attracted key psychoanalytical figures from around the world, including Hug-Hellmuth (who ran the child treatment programme), Ernest Jones, Alix and James Strachey, James Glover (1882–1926) and his younger brother Edward, Sylvia Payne and Ella Sharpe.

Cultural Influences

As well as the intellectual influences we have looked at, there were other events, encounters and relationships that affected the direction and formation of Klein's thinking. Melanie's move to London and her involvement with the British Psychoanalytical Society was to have a huge impact on the psychoanalytical school of thought in general, causing an irreparable split. With the onset of World War II and the arrival of German and Austrian émigrés in Britain, things were to become more uncomfortable and difficult for Klein, leading to her making many enemies and few friends.

During the 1920s, Britain's economy initially flourished, as the manufacturing and construction industries grew rapidly to rebuild the nation post-World-War I. However, by the end of the decade, things were very different. Interest rates were high, and the gap between rich and poor widened, leading to strikes and the 1930s depression. The feeling in London at that time was not, as in Europe, one of trying to preserve and defend a dying and persecuted culture, but quite the opposite: of challenging and often ridiculing any sort of tradition. The 1914–18 war had highlighted the aggressive, animal instincts so well hidden in polite society and enticed those with curious minds to explore these dark places. Writers such as Virginia Woolf and Marie Stopes were women at their own frontiers of discovery, courageously going where no man had been before. It was into this setting that Klein first stepped when she arrived in Britain in 1926 at the invitation of Ernest Jones.

Jones already had an interest in pre-oedipal functioning, which he would write about in his paper 'The Origin and Structure of the Superego' (1926), and which was at odds with Freud's theories, bringing him more in line with Klein's ideas. However, Jones was skilled in diplomacy and adept at maintaining his relationship with Freud while challenging the 'phallocentricism' (his term) of Freudian developmental theory.

Jones invited Klein to speak at the British Psychoanalytical Society, where members initially believed that her psychoanalytic language, theories and interpretations were the same as her German and Austrian peers. The British analysts, clearly unaware of the clash between Klein and the Berlin Society members, were therefore convinced that discussions held between them and Klein were based upon true Freudian theory.

However, with the horrors of World War II and the subsequent arrival of the Jewish émigrés, largely helped by Ernest Jones, Klein's relationships within the Society were about to be disrupted. It wasn't long before the Society found itself reconfigured into two main groups: the Kleinians and the Freudians, with a third refusing to place allegiance. Jones, as President, was in a particularly difficult situation as he was a personal friend of the Freuds but also Klein's advocate.

Fig. 4 Ernest Jones, Melanie Klein and Anna Freud (date unknown).

Anna Freud

Freud's daughter, Anna, was to have a marked effect on Klein's work. It was not that Anna's own theories influenced Klein, but that their strong dislike of one another meant that Klein was often forced to strengthen her ideas in order to defend her work in opposition to Anna.

Anna entered psychoanalysis with her father and began to pursue an interest in his work and writings. She was first placed under the guidance of Hug-Hellmuth, then began her own analysis of children, and by 1925 was teaching at the Vienna Training Institute on the technique. Her first book, *An Introduction to the Technique of Child Analysis* (1927) completely clashed with Klein's theories. Anna Freud's theory was that 'in children's analysis the transference plays a different role... and the analyst not only 'represents mother' but is still an original second mother in the life of the child'. This became the standard view in child analysis.

Anna and her family fled Austria in 1938 and moved to England. In 1941 she founded the Hampstead War Nursery for children affected by the war. Many members of staff were also Austro-German émigrés and were trained in psychoanalytic theory and practice. Her observations on how stress affected children when they were apart from their parents and relationships they formed as substitutes were later published in her *Normality and Pathology in Childhood* (1965). One of her major contributions was establishing how attachment disruptions affect later psychological developments. Most of her work, however, focused on her father's work, tightening his theories on the developmental stages and defence mechanisms.

Klein and the Freuds at War

Klein's cold war with the Freuds began back in 1927. When Anna Freud read her paper 'The Theory of Children's Analysis' at the Tenth Psycho-Analytical Congress in Innsbruck that September, it was viewed as an open attack on Klein's theories on early child analysis and transference. Anna vehemently opposed these ideas, and she openly attacked Klein's interpretive methods. Anna Freud insisted that winning the child's confidence was the primary aim: negative feelings towards the analyst were 'essentially inconvenient'. The role of the analyst should be confined to an educational influence, she said. (Interestingly, Freud himself argued against the idea that a child could be harmed by interpretations of his unconscious, as documented in the case of Little Hans). Anna also openly mocked Klein's play technique, saying 'if a child knocks a lamp-post' Klein interprets the action as aggressive tendencies towards the father, while it could just have been something innocuous that just happened to occur one day.

Klein, distressed, begged Jones for a chance to answer Anna's charges, to which he agreed. She responded indignantly that Anna missed the point: only if the play was accompanied by feelings of anxiety or guilt would she interpret the unconscious. Used properly, it led to the Oedipus Complex, which she saw ensuing from the process of weaning at the end of the second year, going completely against Freud's developmental theories. The aim of analysis, Klein believed, was to put the patient in touch with reality and assuage the harsh Superego, which not only exists in an infant already (rather than developing from the resolution of the Oedipal Complex) but has buried the original objects (parents) of the Oedipal drama in 'imagos' or internal representations. Klein compares her six-year-old patient Erna with Anna Freud's 'seven-year-old neurotically naughty little girl'. Rather than explore the unconscious, Anna Freud tried to persuade her patient that she couldn't possibly hate her mother who clearly loves her so much. For Klein, Erna's naughtiness arose from guilt and a need for punishment for her early oral and anal-sadistic fixations, so her approach was to manage the Superego's vehemence.

Jones rose to defend Klein in a show of supporting fair-mindedness and questioning Anna's approach in a series of letters. Sigmund Freud was famously touchy, and Jones' letters usually begin with a lengthy flattery before moving in for the kill. Jones postulated that Anna's resistances lay in her own incomplete analysis, which of course was carried out by her father.

In a letter to Jones, Sigmund Freud fumes, 'the view of Mrs Klein about the behaviour of the Ego-ideal (Superego) in children seems completely impossible to me and stands in contradiction to all my basic assumptions' (31 May 1927). Jones responded:

> *'The only difference I was aware of is that she dates both the Oedipus conflict and the genesis of the Superego a year or two earlier than you have...As one of your chief discoveries has been the fact that young children are much more mature than had been generally supposed both sexually and morally, I had regarded the conclusions reached from Frau Klein's experiences as being simply a direct continuation of your own.'* (Letter from Jones to Sigmund Freud, 20 June 1927)

Some have argued that while Freud seems to ignore Klein's ideas, she may have caused him to revise some of his theories. In *Inhibitions, Symptoms and Anxiety* (1925) he reverses his idea that anxiety results from repression, now seeing it as a defence employed by the Ego. In *Civilization and its Discontents* (1930), he connects the Superego with the child's own innate aggression. He wrote: 'I can no longer understand how we could have overlooked the ubiquity of non-erotic aggressivity and destructiveness and have failed to give it its due place in our interpretation of life'. But while their ideas increasingly cross-fertilized, the presence of Anna ensured Sigmund and Melanie would never achieve a rapport.

Extraordinary and Controversial

At a British Society meeting in 1940, Anna Freud, Edward Glover and the Viennese accused Klein's work of not being psychoanalysis but a 'sublimation' of it (Klein was in Scotland at the time, Jones in the country, and Glover running the British Society). This gave rise to a series of Scientific Meetings – later known as the Extraordinary Meetings (starting in February 1942) followed by the Controversial Discussions (which continued for four years until 1946) – whereby, effectively, Kleinians were expected to defend their theories and present scientific proof to the furious Freudians.

In 1943, Susan Isaacs presented a paper (taking long-distance written instruction from Klein) that offered proof of the early defence mechanisms and phantasies of a child's inner life through case studies, contending that Melanie Klein and Anna Freud's views were not that different. The British psychoanalyst Ronald Fairbairn (1889–1964), who had been greatly influenced by Klein since the 1930s, also presented a paper, stating that 'inner reality thus becomes the scene of situations involving relationships between the Ego and the internal objects'.

Anna Freud, however, steadfastly refused to accept the existence of psychic life before the second year. Breasts weren't internalized and split into good and bad, Superegos weren't persecutory or even formed until the age of six. Her argument was unusually eloquent. In it she stated that the infant, rather than attacking and desiring the mother, is only concerned about its own wellbeing and gratification.

In May 1942, during the Extraordinary Meetings, Klein telephoned Anna Freud and suggested they meet to resolve their differences; in the next meeting, Anna Freud coldly stated that a desire for reconciliation was a sign of weakness and insecurity. Melitta was of course present and virulently opposed to Klein, but was, it would seem, mostly ignored – probably due to her attacks being largely personal rather than theoretical. In June, it was decided that the Child Seminars for students be divided equally between Anna Freud, Melanie Klein and Donald Winnicott (1896–1971), in effect outlining the eventual divide within the society: the Freudians, the Kleinians, and the British Independents.

In 1944, Melanie Klein attended the discussions to argue for the death instinct, which many Freudians didn't believe in. Klein's theory was a lifelong fusing of the life and death instincts, both in a continual battle for supremacy. In a similar vein, the final proposals that ended the discussions agreed to the introduction of two parallel courses, Kleinian and Freudian. On team Anna Freud were Dorothy Burlingham (1891–1979), Kate Friedlander (1902–49), Barbara Low (1877–1955) and Ella Sharpe. Team Klein included Joan Riviere, Paula Heimann (1899–1982), Susan Isaacs and Sylvia Payne. A few crucial members, including Donald Winnicott, Michael Balint, Ronald Fairbairn, Marion Milner (1900–98) and John Bowlby (1907–90) formed the Middle Group, which would eventually become The Independents. Many of these would go on to form the Object Relations School. Amazingly, the British School has managed to survive with this split until today.

It is striking that both Anna Freud and Melanie Klein were unwanted younger children whose fathers preferred their elder sisters. Perhaps the former merely lacked the dominating presence of a Libussa to incorporate into her theory. Psychoanalyst John Bowlby later commented that the two women were mirror images of each other, albeit one charismatic, vain and formidable, the other shy and retiring. He also added that while Anna worshipped at the shrine of Sigmund, Melanie worshipped at the shrine of Melanie Klein.

3. Splitting

'The Ego is incapable of splitting the object – internal or external – without a corresponding splitting taking place within the Ego.' (Klein, quoted in Holmes, 1992)

In Melanie Klein's theory, 'splitting' is a primary defence mechanism that occurs from birth and throughout life, internally and externally. Along with Projective Identification (see Chapter 4) it is one of the cornerstones of Kleinian analysis. In young children, splitting is seen as part of normal development as well as a way of managing unbearable anxiety that arises when a baby experiences ambivalence or complexity. These are both intolerable to a child; they like certainty, such as the absolute heroes and monsters of fairy tales. Characters (and people) that are seen as 100 per cent good, or 100 per cent bad. When faced with a person acting in two different ways (a caregiver may be relaxed and easy-going one day, but angry on another), the baby simply decides there must be two different people. It 'splits' the person into (for example) 'good dad' and 'bad dad' in its mind.

However, adults can also revert to splitting as a defence. For example, when life or a relationship (with a love 'object') becomes overwhelmingly complex and beyond our control, we often simplify things and people by deciding to designate them as 'good' or 'bad', and view them with love or hate, rather than attempting to comprehend the possibility of a fusion of both. In extreme cases, we endeavour to create a chasm between the designated good and bad objects – think of Trump's wall, Brexit, acrimonious divorce, or a deliberate severance between our civilized minds and ill-behaved bodies, where we might start to 'live in our heads' and numb ourselves against difficult emotions felt in the body by self-medicating with food or drugs.

Klein was not the first person to come up with the concept of psychological splitting. There are recordings of cases of split-personality as far back as 1586, the most famous being German doctor Eberhardt Gmelin's case study of 'exchanged personalities' in 1791. In 1886, writer Robert Louis Stevenson captured the internal conflict of the Victorian era in his story *The Strange Case of Dr Jekyll and Mr Hyde*, where civilized man and his bestial nature are separated into two distinct personalities within one person. Jekyll explicitly recognizes the dual nature of a human being, lamenting that 'Man is not truly one, but truly two'.

Around the same time, in France's Salpêtrière Hospital, doctors Jean-Martin Charcot and Pierre Janet (1859–1947) began to discover links between hysteria in patients and split-off (sometimes multiple) personalities. Picking up on Charcot and Janet's work, Austrian physicians Josef Breuer and Sigmund Freud wrote a joint paper suggesting that 'The splitting of consciousness...is present in every hysteria, and that a tendency to such a dissociation, and with it the emergence of abnormal states of consciousness...is the basic phenomenon of this neurosis' (Breuer & Freud, 1893).

Charcot, and later Breuer, discovered through hypnosis that their patients who presented as fragmented or hysterical had often split off memories of early sexual abuse, so that the memories were no longer accessible to the conscious mind. Charcot, Janet and Breuer later worked together to form the basis of our knowledge of multiple-personality disorder, now known as Dissociative Identity Disorder or DID. The term 'schizophrenia' was coined by Eugen Bleuler in 1908 from Ancient Greek σχίζω (skhízō, 'to split') and φρήν (phrēn, 'mind, heart, diaphragm').

Jung too used the vocabulary of split-off parts and sub-personalities, which would be subsumed into the work of modern therapists working with trauma today. Think of Richard Schwartz's Internal Family Systems (IFS) model where, as in systemic family theory, clients can explore their inner worlds as peopled with various personalities, all operating dynamically to keep the Self safe. Or dissociation (what Charcot termed '*la belle indifférence*' – the ability to shut off the memories that cause us pain). This is a splitting of the mind from the body to disconnect our sensations and emotions from our awareness (as explored today by trauma experts such as Daniel Siegel, Judith Herman and Bessel van der Kolk). Many of these ideas are now backed by studies in neuroscience.

Today, childhood sexual abuse and rape are more openly talked about in the media due to major public exposés such as the Jimmy Savile (UK) and Harvey Weinstein (USA) cases, yet traumatic responses such as splitting remain little understood. 'Why didn't they come forward at the time?', is still a common response by the media, courts and the general public.

Back in the late 19th and early 20th centuries, the idea that incestual abuse might be a relatively common occurrence was intolerable to physicians and society at large. It was definitely something that society did not want to think about (and therefore it was shut down and split off from its consciousness). Charcot's theories of hysteria were later refuted, and French psychiatry remained on the fringes of the psychoanalytical movement. Freud initially agreed that hysterics 'suffer mainly from reminiscences' (*Studies on Hysteria*, 1895) and that these women (and a few men) had been sexually molested. These unconscious memories of early childhood sexual abuse resulted in hysterical or obsessional symptoms, according to Freud, which might be cured when the memories became consciously known (i.e. no longer split off from the mind). This idea is echoed in the work of today's trauma expert Bessel van der Kolk (b.1943), who examined the ways this happened in his book, *The Body Keeps the Score* (2014). However, when Freud presented this idea to the Psychoanalytic Society, they threatened to eject him from the society rather than accept his theory, and so Freud declared the hysteric was *remembering a phantasy* incest, from the Oedipal stage, not a real one. This idea could be more easily held by his colleagues, but it is thought by many to have delayed progress in the therapeutic field of trauma for many decades.

For Klein, the trauma goes back to birth itself. Splitting, she said, begins as soon as the infant is thrust unwittingly into the world in an act of profound violence, immediately torn between a desire to return to the womb and a need to attach to the world to survive. From then on, it is a dynamic and ongoing process to separate good from bad, love from hate, life from death. Primary splitting is not a malfunction of a personality (although it can manifest as such in later life), according to Klein, but the basis of the Ego itself.

The Paranoid-Schizoid Position

Klein's theory of primary splitting arose though her work as a child psychoanalyst. She saw in children a constant struggle between an urge to destroy their objects (toys) and a desire to preserve them. Playing with toys became seen by Klein as an expression of the dynamic inner workings and conflicts of a child's mind. In Klein's interpretations, the toys acted as symbols of the primary objects in the child's life – mother, father, siblings – but they also stood for body parts, faeces, fluids and unborn children. Play was often a process of separation and reparation; destruction and reparation; disintegration and unsatisfactory attempts at integration; even as all the while the anxiety about the destructive instinct that existed in the first place remained firmly in place.

Fig. 5 Toys used by Melanie Klein

Klein believed that in play, a child enacts unresolved internal conflicts from its infancy. She paid closer attention to the narrative of play and interpreted what the toys stood for. Drawing on Freud's studies of the unconscious, she became aware that these could be the 'imprints on the mind' of infantile feelings.

> *'Infantile feelings and phantasies leave, as it were, their imprints on the mind, imprints which do not fade away but get stored up, remain active and exert a continuous and powerful influence on the emotional and intellectual life of the individual... I believe that [phantasy-building] is the most primitive mental activity and that phantasies are in the mind of the infant almost from birth.'* (Klein, 1936)

Phantasy, for Klein, is key to understanding the mind. Freud believed that an infant's mind is a *tabula rasa*, or blank slate, that forms from biological drives to survive, procreate and seek pleasure, taking many years to fully form. Klein, in contrast, believed that Ego formation begins from the moment the infant is born, and saw the first three months of life as being rich with phantasies so horrific and extreme that many have compared it to the paintings by Hieronymus Bosch. And for the baby, existing in a state of primary narcissism, these phantasies are experienced as reality.

Klein later called the developmental stage of the first three months 'the Paranoid-Schizoid position', during which the tiny baby is busy defending against intolerable persecutory anxieties using psychic processes of splitting alongside projection and introjection, which we shall explore in the next chapter. The

Paranoid-Schizoid state, as we shall see, is more self-centred and ruthless than Sigmund and Anna Freud's pleasure-seeking primary narcissism.

A Matter of Death and Life

Splitting, according to Klein, begins at birth, from the moment the infant is wrenched cruelly from the womb into a bright, chaotic and confusing new world. This, she believed, triggered the emergence of the Freudian death instinct (a theory he later dropped). In response to the trauma of birth, the child is filled with annihilating rage, a desire 'to die, to sleep'. But an encounter with the life-giving part-object, the breast, triggers the life instinct, the introjection of warmth, love and life-preserving milk. Thus, the eternal conflict begins. As British psychoanalyst Hanna Segal (1918–2011) describes:

> *'To me the death instinct is not a biological drive to return to the inorganic (as Freud described it) but it is a psychological wish to annihilate this sudden change brought about by birth. So, the infant is born into a sort of chaos of contradictory perceptions – pleasant and unpleasant – and of contradictory desires; very soon he starts to sort them out and the sorting out is called "splitting".'* (Miller, 1983)

The life and death instincts begin their dance of conflict and fusion, which continues throughout life. The presence of death and negative emotions at the heart of Klein's work is what many of her colleagues found intolerable. British psychoanalyst Jacqueline Rose (b.1949) compares the negativity in Klein to

Stephen Hawking's black hole theory (Rose, 1993). The idea that a baby is not born good and innocent but filled with hate and rage is experienced by many people as intolerable, and is particularly denied by humanist therapies and psychoanalysts who follow the different reasoning of Anna Freud. It causes anxiety and it creates splits, as it did within the British Psychoanalytical Society.

As with some of her earlier theories, Klein thought she was merely expanding on ideas first created by her idol, Sigmund Freud. He had briefly explored the death instinct in 'Instincts and their Vicissitudes' (1915). It helped him explain things that could not be explained by his theory of libidinous drives, such as resistance in therapy or aggressive tendencies. Later Freud concluded that the fear of death was a fear of castration, which Klein contested in 'The Theory of Anxiety and Guilt' (1948). Freud did not believe that a baby is aware of death, or anything much, whereas Klein believed that an unconscious awareness of death is present from birth, to which the response is a 'fear of annihilation of life' (Klein, 1932). We are driven not by sexual impulses and biological urges to procreate, she said, but by fear of death and the will to destroy. 'Hate…', Freud wrote in 1915, 'as a relation to Objects, is older than love. It derives from the narcissistic Ego's primordial repudiation of the external world with its out-pouring stimuli.' Freud did not develop his theory of life and death instincts, because he could not prove they had a scientific basis, whereas Klein made them central to her work (Rosenfeld, 1971).

Good Breast, Bad Breast

In 1946, Klein wrote, 'I have often expressed my view that object-relations exist from the beginning of life, the first object being the mother's breast, which to the child becomes split into a good (gratifying) and bad (frustrating) breast: this splitting results in a severance of love and hate' (Klein, 1946). While Freud's theories are based on biological drives and instincts that ensure the survival of the species, Klein's are rooted in a more basic survival instinct – to attach, and to receive nourishment and warmth in order to thrive. To put it simply, Freud was all about the penis, Klein about the breast.

Vulnerable and helpless, a new born baby does not see 'people' but shapes and objects, with which it develops a very basic relationship to get its survival needs met. A new born infant doesn't know that its mother is a human being, let alone a complex, contradictory one with her own needs. At first, the only thing that matters is the breast (a part-object – it is part of a larger object). The breast is either feeding the baby (good breast), giving nourishment, warmth, love and life, or not feeding and disappearing altogether (bad breast) causing hunger, pain and potential destruction (Klein, 'On Weaning', 1936).

Milk from the good breast is life-giving and warming, goodness that the baby physically ingests and emotionally 'introjects' (takes inside of itself; see Chapter 4) as an imago (an internalized symbol of the good breast/mother). This is the beginning of object relations and the basis of Ego formation. 'The first internal good object acts as a focal point in the Ego,' said Klein (1946). But all the while we have to bear in mind, as Jacqueline Rose has argued, that the baby already contains a black hole of negative emotion (Rose, 1992).

In the baby's 'phantasy' interpretation, the bad breast isn't just off having a rest or running a business, but deliberately hurting and persecuting the baby, causing actual physical stabbing sensations in its stomach that feel aggressive and murderous. A baby does not understand absence and loss, it merely experiences them as bad. The baby hates the bad breast so much, it wants to bite and hurt the breast (a theory Klein came across in the work of her mentor, Karl Abraham).

Its own aggressive tendencies terrify the baby. Fully immersed in its phantasy view of the world, it believes it really did destroy the breast. The breast that returns must be the good breast, restoring love and goodness to the baby. Yet the baby is aware that it also contains bad, destructive aspects and wants to keep this as far away as possible from its good part in case it destroys that, too. The personality splits. The baby is good and bad but cannot accept that both can exist in the same space together. Splitting is the baby's first attempt at trusting and loving. By separating good from bad, the infant has the chance to experience total goodness, which it takes in (introjects) as a base for its sense of self. On the opposite side of the same coin, it also experiences persecution from the bad object and in response feels itself to be bad.

Klein wrote that 'The Ego is incapable of splitting the object – internal and external – without a corresponding splitting taking place within the Ego... The more sadism prevails in the process of incorporating the object, and the more the object is felt to be in pieces, the more the Ego is in danger of being split' (Klein, 1946).

The aggressive feelings are now part of the baby's Ego formation: it feels the bad inside itself. But now the baby begins to worry that the bad inside will attack or destroy the good inside: it must keep them far apart. How it does this seems extraordinary, employing a kind of abstract symbolization and constant flow of motion, a perpetual process of splitting, projection and introjection in order to assuage its anxiety. Good and bad, love and hate, life and death are not only split but kept far apart in the baby's internal and external phantasy – the breast and eventually the mother and father – so that good is kept intact, uncontaminated, safe. Mentally juggling to save your life is not exactly restful, hence the anxiety is not calmed but remains latent, watchful.

Healthy Ego development, as Klein regularly pointed out, relies on the introjection of goodness as the basis of the Ego. If the baby does not experience enough love and nourishment (forming a disordered attachment, for example), it will not only fail to thrive but will be overwhelmed by its persecutory anxieties, causing the Ego to fragment (as seen in schizophrenic patients).

In healthy development, these defensive strategies eventually resolve and integrate as the infant grows and begins to understand the world, to accept its complexities and grey areas, and to see that its mother is a separate, complex individual who is both loving and sometimes absent. There is a sense of loss and melancholia that accompanies this awakening (see Chapter 5: The Depressive Position), but splitting is an ongoing process. 'As the adaptation to the external world increases, this splitting is carried out on planes which gradually become increasingly nearer and nearer to reality.' If a child successfully finds 'a way out of the conflict between love and uncontrollable hatred and sadism,' it can develop a happy relationship to its real mother. 'Gradually, by unifying and then splitting up the good and bad, the phantastic and the real, the external and internal objects, the Ego makes its way towards a more realistic conception of both the external and internal objects and thus obtains a satisfactory relation to both.' (Klein, 'Psychogenesis of Manic-Depressive States', 1935).

Envy and the Baby

One of Klein's most controversial theories was centred on envy, which she presented to the British Psychoanalytical Society in 1957 to the consternation of many of her followers. The baby, said Klein, is not only filled with rage against the bad breast for persecuting it through deprivation. It also feels envy for the good breast because it symbolizes intolerable separation and challenges the baby's phantasy of omnipotence. The good breast represents post-natal life, which the death instinct is compelled to destroy, and the baby does so by biting and devouring. The primal splitting of good and bad is further complicated by envy.

Envy is unbearable for the infant Ego, so becomes split off. Klein believed envy often remains unexpressed in analysis but exerts influence in preventing the process of integration. One example is in transference, the devaluing of the psychoanalyst's work. Karl Abraham connected hostility and aggression in adult narcissists with the presence of envy – a need to triumph over the analyst, an inability to tolerate the superiority of anyone else. Everything is everyone else's fault and the person in this state, baby or adult, has no sense of personal responsibility, even though it attempts to control its misbehaving objects in phantasy. Externalized envy aimed at outside objects simultaneously wreaks havoc on our internalized states and basic self-worth.

Another way the baby tries to deal with envy is through greed – if it takes enough good breast milk and internalizes it, it can create its own internal supply and cease to need the breast any more. Of course, this absolute self-sufficiency is never achieved, and the greedy personality is never satiated.

Reparation

As the baby grows, it becomes aware that the breast belongs to a woman who it can interact with, who has a separate personality (see Winnicott and Bowlby, who further explored these early interactions in object relations and attachment theory). The realization that we are alone and separate and can never really know another fully creates feelings of loss and sadness, which Klein called the 'Depressive Position' (see Chapter 5). It is also key to healthy integration, she said. In her paper 'On the Sense of Loneliness' (1963) she wrote: 'Together with the urge to split there is from the beginning of life the drive towards integration.' The splitting processes which are designed to counteract insecurity are never enough, therefore the Ego has to come to terms with its own destructive impulses, tempering them with love. Integration of split-off parts is often the aim in psychotherapies today, even if, as British psychoanalyst Wilfred Bion (1897–1979) warns, integration can be felt as catastrophic change.

Klein observed in her young patients a drive to reparation, which she describes in *Love, Guilt and Reparation* (Riviere & Klein, 1937). The guilt that arises from envy and aggression triggers a drive to repair the damage. The drive to reparation is a form of hope that can keep despair at bay and is for Klein an essential part of the ability to love. The capacity to love also depends on the protection and preservation of the good objects; splitting keeps our loved objects safe.

Subject Relation to Object Relationships

Klein calls her theory 'object relations', but it is not the mutual loop of intersubjectivity that we know as object relations today.

Lavinia Gomez (1997) prefers to name Klein's version 'subject relations', because the baby seems to be entirely responsible for its own Ego development. For Klein, the mother is passive, an object onto which the baby projects its anxieties and happiness, and its love and hate (rather like the traditional psychoanalyst). One of the criticisms often levelled at Klein is that she is simply projecting her anxieties into the child and her patients, that it is not the baby having these feelings, but the mother/analyst who cannot tolerate feelings of envy and hatred towards her child. (Klein suffered with post-natal depression, and some analysts have pointed out that her theory of envy can easily be read as a barely-veiled missive to her vengeful daughter.)

Klein's student Donald Winnicott would return these negative and complex emotions and desires to the mother. His famous list of things a mother secretly wants to do to her baby include eating the baby and having sex with the baby (the flood of oxytocin – the love hormone – to the brain as the baby sucks at the breast and the milk is 'let down'). Winnicott is often accused of sugaring Klein's pill: the good and bad mother combines in his theory to become 'good enough', creating a sense of safety for the baby that allows it to develop healthily.

But is it really that simple? How can we possibly know the mind of a baby? Perhaps neuroscience will eventually give us answers. Perhaps Klein's theories tell us more about the mind of a mother, forced to carry the enormous responsibility and terrifying awareness of life and death from that moment of conception, often on her own, often persecuted by society if she is seen to fail. As Jaqueline Rose and other feminist writers have pointed out, mothers (particularly single, immigrant, teenage, poor, aborting mothers) are often the split-off parts of society, because we cannot tolerate anything other than the sanitized, simplified, fluffy version of our beginning.

4. Projective Identification

The definition of Projective Identification, according to the Melanie Klein Trust today, is as follows: 'Projective Identification is an unconscious phantasy in which aspects of the self or an internal object are split off and attributed to an external object.' Klein first coined the term in her paper 'Notes on some Schizoid Mechanisms' in 1946, in which she concluded that as the infant turns its libidinal and aggressive impulses and phantasies towards the mother, 'harmful excrements, expelled in hatred, (together with) split-off parts of the Ego are projected onto the mother or, as I would rather call it, *into* the mother'. (Klein added a footnote here, explaining that projecting 'into' another person was the 'only way of conveying the unconscious process I am trying to describe'.) She says that in this way, the hatred the infant feels against parts of its self is now directed toward the mother, and crucially, 'This leads to a particular form of identification which establishes the prototype of an aggressive object-relation'. Six years later, Klein added, 'I suggest for these processes the term "Projective Identification"'.

This term has since become one of the key concepts of the psychoanalytical relationship and is seen as a primary defence enacted by the client that allows the analyst to fully emotionally and physically experience the client's split-off parts. If it remains undetected and is not fully worked through, Projective Identification can cause problems for the client, analyst and the therapeutic relationship.

The Route to Knowledge

Projective Identification can sound a bit mystical – and indeed Hanna Segal calls it Klein's 'meta-psychological theory' – but many psychoanalysts and psychotherapists view it as the basis of counter-transference, a form of deep empathy and a vital communication from the client's unconscious. Wilfred Bion described Projective Identification as the single most important phenomenon in individual psychotherapy (Ogden, 2005).

However, for Klein it was not part of a reciprocal, intersubjective therapeutic process that many therapists and analysts use today, but a primary defence mechanism, alongside spitting, projection and introjection – all of which are used with the aim of alleviating intense anxiety. While it is generally believed the concept of counter-transference originated with Klein and was later developed by Bion as a key concept in Object Relations, Klein herself felt that counter-transference got in the way of the analysis (Grosskurth, 1987).

Defences Against the Death Instinct

Projective Identification, according to Klein, is employed by babies in the first three months of life, during which they are absorbed in a phantasy world of relating to external objects. Klein called this stage of development the Paranoid-Schizoid position. Far from living in blissful ignorance, a newborn baby, she said, is governed by extreme anxiety triggered by the presence of the death instinct, which it attempts to manage and evade with some psychological juggling that Klein identified as splitting, projection, introjection and – in her later work – Projective Identification. The infant *introjects* (literally 'takes in') the goodness and love of its mother's milk and then projects this loving goodness onto 'the good breast'. In order to keep its internalized good objects safe, the baby splits off and projects intolerable parts of its self, such as the oral-sadistic instinct to destroy the good breast.

The Paranoid-Schizoid position is, for Kleinians, a normal stage of development, which flows into the Depressive Position and eventual healthy integration. However, if development is impaired in some way, these methods of relating to and defending against the object remain. Klein believed schizophrenic patients were trapped in the Paranoid-Schizoid position, in the same way that manic-depressive (bipolar) patients are caught in the Depressive Position (see Chapter 5). Integrated adults had worked through these stages in the first year of life and were therefore able to have healthy object relations.

Introjection

Projection and Introjection were already common currency in psychoanalytical theory when Klein was developing her own theories. Introjection was used to describe the internalization of good and bad objects through a form of identification and/or ingesting. For Freud, the Ego and Superego are constructed by absorbing behaviour patterns into the personality. A loved person becomes part of someone's identity, and you may see them displaying characteristics of that person who has been taken inside; we may even find ourselves saying things like 'I am turning into my father'. At age three or four, a child stops seeing its parents as sexual objects and internalizes them: they become part of the personality, the Superego.

Karl Abraham observed that disturbed patients became more preoccupied with taking things inside themselves, often through biting or eating, either in dreams or phantasies. He noted that introjection was an oral stage process, and loss (defecation) an anal process.

As Klein wrote in her paper 'Weaning' (1936), only a part of the gratification of being fed results from the alleviation of hunger: another part is the pleasure the baby feels suckling at its mother's breast, the warm sensation of the milk running down the throat and filling the stomach. This creates the felt sense of goodness and love inside; the first experience of taking in or introjecting goodness. The breast is therefore the source of this nourishment, of life itself, and this source, internalized, becomes the core of the baby's Ego. If a child has introjected enough goodness as the basis of its Ego, it will better be able to repair and integrate conflicts with more destructive parts. If it doesn't have enough experience of goodness, it could revert to excessive splitting and Projective Identification, leading to a fragmented, unboundaried Ego.

Projection

Freud wrote that drives and desires that a person cannot accept as their own are placed outside the self, projected or displaced onto other people or the world. For example, if you hate someone, but your Ego cannot tolerate you as a person who hates, you may project your feelings onto the object of your hatred and instead accuse them of hating you. Projection isn't reality, but the person projecting can believe it is the truth, as though they can mind-read (they know what the other person is feeling), while the person being projected onto may have no idea what is happening. Freud's focus was more on transference, displacement and sublimation. Projection as a defence mechanism was developed by Freud's daughter Anna, in *The Ego and the Mechanisms of Defence* (1936), although she opposed the notion that a young child is capable of employing defence mechanisms, let alone transference, and insisted that children needed to be treated differently from adults in analysis.

Klein, however, felt that projection begins at birth with the projection of the death instinct, the negative and destructive feelings triggered by the trauma of birth, and the frustration and agonies of hunger. A baby cannot conceive of others who may feel the same way it does: it is, in this state of primary narcissism, feeling omnipotent but in reality helpless, therefore operating on a phantasy level.

The baby sometimes experiences the breast as good and loving, said Klein, and at other times as a bad, persecutory object that frustrates its desire to feed, causing it intense pain and potential death. Since a baby cannot hold two apparently opposing impulses, in its phantasy it divides the breast into good (feeding) and bad (absent). In order that the bad cannot annihilate or contaminate the good, it keeps them far apart, by splitting off negative aspects of its own Ego and projecting them out onto the world or object.

Later, Klein added that the baby also experiences envy of the breast responsible for its happiness. This instigates a desire to introject the entire object so that it no longer relies on the whim of the breast for nourishment but controls it from within. When this greed is frustrated, the baby has phantasies of attacking and biting the breast that feeds it, which later gives rise to guilt (see Chapter 5: The Depressive Position). But in the Paranoid-Schizoid position, its intolerable attacks on the breast are split-off and projected to become persecutory objects, which cause the baby deeper anxiety and a greater need to introject more goodness.

The baby also projects good parts of its Ego, sometimes idealizing the mother or breast. This is another way of alleviating anxiety, as good breast/mother will always love, feed and protect her baby. The mother who may be tired or irritable or depressed is treated as a separate object, the perfect host for the baby's projected negative or aggressive tendencies. It is the negative feelings of hate and aggression already present in the Kleinian baby that people (including many of her greatest admirers) find hard to swallow.

From Splitting to Projective Identification

Projective Identification takes projection one stage further. Rather than projecting unwanted split-off parts onto the object as though onto a blank screen, then either idealizing them or feeling persecuted, Projective Identification is the phantasy of projecting a part of oneself *into* the other person or object. The split-off parts become phantasized as having taken possession of the mother's body and *she becomes identified with them*.

There is another aspect that separates Projective Identification from simple projection. In projection, the split-off part is disowned, separate, to be defended against – as in racism and homophobia. The person projecting may feel estranged, bewildered or threatened by the object of the projection (Ogden, 1979). In Projective Identification there is a blurring of boundaries. The object being projected into is an extension of the baby, therefore in his omnipotent phantasy, *it can be controlled by him*. And indeed, through subtle manipulations, the recipient can be made to feel and act in accordance with the projective phantasy.

American psychoanalyst Thomas Ogden (b.1946), who has written comprehensively about Projective Identification, describes the following scenario. Imagine a child is frightened by his desire to destroy someone who opposes or frustrates him. He could project this feeling into his mother and encourage her to feel more aggressive by frustrating her attempts to dress, feed or toilet train him. A mother who has not come to terms with her own destructive wishes may struggle to deal with or 'contain' (Bion, 1962) these feelings. She may blame the child, or herself, lash out, withdraw, or displace her feelings onto other family members and objects.

In adults, this may happen through enactments during normal conversation, through subtle cues, triggers and manipulations. By acting victimized, for example, you can cast the other into the role of the persecutor. You may accuse your partner of being unhappy without owning your own unhappiness. Often the object is unaware that the feelings they are experiencing are not their own. Equally, the person projecting will be unaware that the other has absorbed their feelings but may themselves feel empty and depleted.

When we listen empathically, we sometimes tune into deeper, hidden emotions that the other person has split-off and denied or buried in themselves. When a client is talking about a traumatic experience in a flat voice, the therapist may be empathically picking up strong emotional reactions that are not being expressed. The therapist feels the client's feelings, but as they are unexpressed or unacknowledged, they become entwined with the therapist's own. It also happens in everyday life: people speak of friends who dump their emotions on them and leave feeling fine, while the person 'dumped on' feels wretched. It is very common in close relationships where, for example, one person unwittingly becomes the other's 'jealousy' or their 'controlling mother' in an enactment.

Introjecting Milk, Projecting Excrements

There is a literal basis for the baby's phantasies of introjection and projection. As we have seen, introjection at the oral stage is sucking and eating. Projection is anal stage excretion, or as Klein says, 'expelling dangerous substances (excrements) out of the self and into the mother'. The excrements are bad parts of the self, and since the baby has no concept of anything in the world beyond the breast and mother, never mind nappy bins, in his phantasy the mother has taken his faeces into herself. The excrements are also viewed as gifts, Klein adds. Good projection is essential for the ability to develop good object relations, but too much and the good parts are lost, the baby feels empty, and the mother becomes the 'Ego-ideal'.

When projecting into the mother, the baby feels the mother contains its excrements or bad parts which are meant to not only injure but control the object. 'In so far as the mother comes to contain the bad parts of the self, she is not felt to be a separate individual but is felt to be the bad self', Klein writes in 'Notes on Some Schizoid Mechanisms' (1946). Hatred against parts of the self are re-directed towards the mother, and this leads to the form of identification that establishes the prototype of an aggressive object-relation, that may be felt in later relationships. These processes taken together are 'Projective Identification'.

If the object is not felt to be safe (which it won't, since it is full of bad parts), the baby also fears retaliation, of being stuck and persecuted from within. No wonder Klein felt that persecutory anxiety predominates in the first three months of life.

Winnicott, Bion and Containment

Projective Identification has its positive uses. As with Winnicott's transitional object (such as a much-loved blanket), it alleviates feelings of loneliness and abandonment. When the object (parent) is absent, the baby believes it is still being held inside that object. We do this when parting from a loved one as a way to quell anxiety. But for a child, in the absence of the transitional object, they may develop a need to be constantly with a parent, crying out for attention to literally put themselves into their parent's mind. This can easily descend into neuroticism.

Bion was analyzed by Klein in 1945, and it was he who developed her theory of Projective Identification to incorporate the mother's ability to transform and modify the projected sensations. What the baby cannot stand to feel, the mother can. In other words, the mother becomes a container for the baby's feelings. The baby can then take the modified feelings back into itself, eventually developing an awareness of its own feelings and, eventually thoughts.

Intersubjective therapeutic relationships tend to work more with the early mother–child interaction in mind, and so use the gentler approach as laid out by Bion, Winnicott and indeed Anna Freud. Kleinian and Freudian psychoanalysis, on the other hand, tended towards a more boundaried analyst–patient transaction, where defences were revealed through no-holds-barred insight (as in Klein's analysis with a ten-year-old boy, see Chapter 6). The aim was the same, however: integration of the split-off parts.

Projective Identification and Counter-transference

Klein's concept of Projective Identification is credited with widening the notion of counter-transference, particularly though the work of Bion. Yet, despite planting the seed, Klein remained sceptical about counter-transference, believing it interfered with therapy. If you have feelings about your patient, she said, you should do an immediate self-analysis (Grosskuth, 1987). German psychoanalyst Paula Heimann's paper 'On Counter-transference' (1949) is considered a central tenet of Kleinian theory and an extension of her ideas. Yet she and Klein had a massive falling out over the paper when Heimann presented it at the Zurich Congress that year.

Heimann argues that counter-transference is the patient's unconscious process; as with Projective Identification, the analyst experiences split off parts of the patient and can use this in the work. Borderline or psychotic patients can provoke particularly powerful emotions, and the analyst must attempt to tolerate these feelings rather than acting them out. Heimann wrote that 'the analyst's counter-transference is not only part and parcel of the analytic relationship, but it is the patient's creation, it is a part of the patient's personality' (Carpy, 1989). Winnicott delivered a similar paper in 1947, 'Hate in the Counter-transference', where he suggested the analyst had to be aware of their own capacity to hate their clients, particularly the more complex and difficult ones, in order to subordinate hate in the analysis. Klein, who was becoming more rigid and intolerant in old age, did not approve of these papers or viewpoints. The fact that the British School embraced the concept of counter-transference so eagerly rattled her. Her response was always that whoever was experiencing extreme reactions to their patients and calling it counter-transference simply needed more analysis – to which Winnicott angrily responded: 'We all need more analysis!' (Grosskurth, 1987).

Although most psychotherapists today are comfortable working with counter-transference, Projective Identification is considered to be more controversial. Like counter-transference, its presence in the psychotherapeutic relationship has evolved into an intersubjective process rather than a defence to be interpreted.

Thomas Ogden (b. 1946) describes working with Projective Identification as a three-step process (Ogden, 1975). First there is the phantasy of projecting parts of the self into the other person and controlling them. Then there is the pressure exerted on the recipient to act, feel and think according to the projection. Finally, the projected feelings, after they are psychologically processed by the recipient, are returned to the projector.

In counter-transference, the therapist (or other person in the relationship) experiences similar feelings to the client: it is a form of deep empathy, attuning to someone's feelings and seeing the world though their eyes. In Projective Identification, the therapist identifies with those feelings, absorbing them as part of their own system. Ideally, the therapist or mother will contain the feelings that the client or baby has found so intolerable (Bion, 1962). Or they will work these feelings through, processing them through their own systems, and showing the client or child that there are other ways to tolerate difficult emotions or aspects of themselves (Ogden, 1975).

Recent findings in affective neuroscience have helped us understand the intersubjective nature of Projective Identification, capturing the spontaneous matching of emotional states between patient and client in the process. We are understanding more how Projective Identification occurs, demystifying the process. It begins with the deep empathic form of listening that allows us to enter a person's inner world, but also opens us to Projective Identification.

> 'When we allow ourselves to be receptive to another person, we have the capacity to resonate with the unconscious feelings of that person like a vibrating tuning fork. And when we resonate with those feelings, our whole being is involved – both mind and body.'
> (Greatrex, 2002)

The intimacy of the therapeutic relationship has been shown to be intensely triggering to some clients, who may idealize or distrust the persecutory intrusion of the therapist.

In modern therapies, listening to the counter-transference and working out what belongs to the therapist and what belongs to the client often provides vital clues for the therapist as to how the client experiences the world. Catching the Projective

Identification and untangling it from their own systems gives therapists a clue to the deeper unconscious and sometimes preverbal and pre-symbolic intersubjective experiences. Both are viewed as a profoundly useful form of communication from the unconscious with the potential to strengthen – or, if missed, harm – the therapeutic relationship. In Projective Identification, the therapist carries the client's feelings, processes them and ideally makes them tolerable and understandable to the client. For this to offer feelings of repair rather than further rupture, the therapist needs to be particularly attuned to how much interpretation and reality the client can bear, perhaps finding creative ways to offer back a 'modified version of what was extruded' (Ogden, 1975). The client can then, perhaps, accept these rejected parts with the same empathy and compassion offered by the therapist, thus enabling integration.

5. The Depressive Position

elanie Klein first wrote about the Depressive Position in 1935. It is a term that she uses to describe the developmental stage that occurs in an infant's first year, after the primal Paranoid-Schizoid Position. She called these two states of mind 'positions' rather than 'stages', because she said that they are not stages we progress through, but positions, or ways of being, that we oscillate between throughout development and into adult life.

The Depressive Position first manifests during weaning – around three to six months – when a child comes to terms with the reality of the world and its place in it. At the heart of the Depressive Position is loss and mourning: mourning the separation of self from the mother, mourning the loss of the phantasy where the child's Ego was the world, mourning the objects it has hurt or destroyed through aggression and envy. But from the ruins there arises first the feeling of guilt, then the drive for reparation and love. In the Depressive Position, a child learns to relate to its objects in a completely new way.

To move into the Depressive Position is not easy or pleasant, as it involves accepting that we are not omnipotent (as we thought) and in fact have very little control; that other people/objects don't revolve around us (as we thought) but instead have their own inner lives and relationships. We also realize that the world and its objects are complex, nuanced and uncertain. As we move into this state of greater clarity, we may occasionally cling to old black-and-white beliefs and Paranoid-Schizoid defence mechanisms. This may also happen to us as adults. This is thought to explain why people who adhere strongly to fundamentalist beliefs (religious, political or other ideological) would rather cling to a belief that they may subconsciously doubt than to develop a tolerance for uncertainty. Sometimes it feels easier to be anxious and angry, to project blame and fear, than to have to experience doubt and loss. And this, according to Klein, is a shift back to the Paranoid-Schizoid position.

At around three months, the Kleinian baby has come to accept that it can survive in this world and becomes less anxious. It has less need for splitting, introjection and projection as defences (see previous chapters) than it did in the first three months. The child begins to view inner and outer reality more accurately. Part-objects are now viewed as whole people, who have their own relationships and feelings; absence is experienced as a loss rather than a persecutory attack. Instead of anger, the baby feels grief. It is at around three months that a baby begins to cry real tears.

From Persecution to Pining and Reparation

Klein first noticed the processes of the Depressive Position by closely observing and interpreting the play and drawings of her young clients, where she saw that the urge to destroy was often followed by the need to repair and restore love. Indeed, the positions in Klein seem to follow a classic drama narrative: a battle of good versus evil, working towards extreme destruction or disintegration, followed by the resolution and reparation of a happy ending.

Klein found, however, that children sometimes force these happy endings before they are ready to let go of the feelings of destruction and aggression that remain, hence the repetitive and obsessive nature of play and creativity.

In her 1940 paper 'Mourning and its Relation to Manic-Depressive States', she notes that she observed similar defences being employed by her manic-depressive patients, and adults going through stages of mourning and grief. She wrote this paper after the death of her son, for which she was attacked and blamed by her daughter. Drawing from the theories of Freud and Abraham on depression and mourning, Klein began to feel that manic-depressive patients were caught in that moment of infantile pre-awareness, employing extremely polarized defences against loss (or 'pining' as Klein calls it) such as the feelings of omnipotence that accompany the highs of mania, and the total self-annihilation of catatonic depression.

For a child, grief is as painful and real as hunger. Idealization and pining for a loved object are important elements of this stage, counteracted with denial and omnipotence. This ambivalence enables the Ego to defend against its 'slavish and perilous dependence on its loved objects' (Klein, 1940). At the same time, the child does not trust its ability to repair and fears destructive sadistic impulses. It wishes instead to triumph over its parents and its internal objects but is constantly reminded of its dependency and needs. The child also begins to collect new experiences of happiness, love and trust, which will enable the development of secure relationships, internally and externally.

This reality-testing is a slow, step-by-step process where the child connects increasingly with the external world and rebuilds its inner world. Klein describes similar processes in mourning, which she believed activated earlier defences: triumph over the dead person, idealization of them, and a sense of possessing them inside. The mourner reality tests the loved object until it returns to a less idealized state, then eases suffering by restoring harmony to its inner world through reparation and love. Thus, suffering becomes sublimated by creativity and wisdom.

Internalizing Lost Objects

The Depressive Position then is the original banishment from the Garden of Eden where the land overflowed with milk and honey. The baby realizes with shock that the people it attacked and hated were the same people as those it loves most and needs. This makes the baby terrified of its anger. Although painful, this sense of loss and guilt is less horrific than the Paranoid-Schizoid fear of total annihilation; the baby still fears for its survival, but this time can relate it to the loss of its primary objects, its parents, and through this recognizes its need for others. The child also fears the loss of his internal good objects; without them he or she would feel bad and unlovable. The internalization of the parents as whole objects – 'imagos' – is a latter stage of the Depressive Position and mourning, where the Ego is rebuilt to accommodate a new reality.

The hallmark of the depressive position is humility, unlike the omnipotence of the Paranoid-Schizoid position. The baby is ejected from the promised land, ashamed of his badness and anger, but determined to win back his parents' love. The humble recognition of guilt gives rise to the capacity in the child for repair and love. The baby learns that although its anger can be damaging, it can also be forgiven, and love can mend the damage.

Depression, Reparation & The Depressive Position

Those who are stuck in depression often feel there is no way out: they lose the trust in themselves to repair the damage done. They may feel their anger is too much; perhaps they have lost sight of their own goodness, or their guilt may be too persecutory and intolerable. This may happen if earlier Paranoid-Schizoid anxieties were only partially resolved, and if life continues to feel persecutory and dangerous.

Young children often play out experiences of persecution, loss, guilt and reparation: tantrums alternate with a need for love and affection, or an urge to give gifts. Early forms of reparation develop into helping and caring behaviour as well as individual interests and talents. Klein saw the capacity for reparation as the basis for creative power and civilized social behaviour.

The Oedipal Complex

Klein controversially placed the Oedipal Stage of a child's development at a much earlier age than Freud and made distinctions between male and female experiences. As we saw in Chapter 2, in Freud the Oedipal Complex is a developmental stage that occurs around age six. As with the Greek myth, the male child is said to want to marry his mother and kill his father; Freud said that these phantasies are kept in check by a castration complex and resolved with the formation of the regulating

Superego. The female child, Freud said, has penis envy instead of a castration complex, and her subsequent loving relationships with men are a healthy sublimation of this.

Klein believed the Oedipal Complex begins much earlier, and that girls and boys have different experiences. Both begin with the mother's breast and the complex reaches its climax around weaning, which (in the Western society in which Klein lived), typically takes place at the end of the child's first year. The child is now seen as ready to tolerate loss, anger and grief – processes it has worked through with the good/bad, nurturing/persecuting, present/absent breast. If weaned too early, Klein said, the child experiences the loss of breast or bottle as a depriving attack, reinforcing the view that the world is hostile. This is because weaning has taken place before the baby has come to terms with less destructive interactions and the power of reparative love.

In her paper 'Oedipal Complex' (1945), Klein said that the baby wants unlimited satisfaction from the breast, and turns in frustration to the father's penis, both 'primary objects of the infant's oral desires'. You may wonder how a baby even knows its father has a penis. According to Klein, all of us are born with a pre-natal unconscious awareness of both the breast and the penis; even if we don't understand what they are, we unconsciously know they symbolize life giving.

As with the breast, the baby also splits its relation to the penis into good and bad and moves between breast and penis in its search for the perfect, ideal object in order to satisfy its craving for love and security. Of course, both are disappointing as they cannot provide endless satisfaction. The primary imagos of breast and penis are introjected into the baby's Ego and form the nucleus of his or her Superego, both protecting and persecutory internal figures. Freud placed the birth of the Superego at around four years old, but Klein believed that only a tiny infant would create such a simplistically sadistic Superego. By four, she felt a child understands moral complexity too well (Klein, 1928).

In the anal stage, the baby's awareness widens. It becomes fixated on the imagined objects of the mother's insides, which in its phantasy contain the father's penis, unborn children/faeces, milk and urine – all good and bad, gifts and weapons, things to be feared and attacked as well as loved and envied. Klein calls this expansion of awareness from mother to the rest of the family the 'circle of loved objects' (Klein, 1945).

From the Paranoid-Schizoid position, the baby views mother and father as a monstrous combination of the above in endless mutual gratification, known as 'The Combined Parent Figure'. The baby projects its rage and envy into this creature, which then becomes even more powerful and evil, threatening its annihilation. It also experiences the figure internally as it has introjected its part-objects.

As Freud had observed in his sessions with five-year-old 'Little Hans' (Freud, 1909), at some point a child may witness actual intercourse between its parents without comprehending what exactly they are seeing. They may interpret it as a frightening act of violence but become confused both by their own biological urges and feelings of loss (or for Klein, envy). The child becomes aware that his parents have a relationship that doesn't involve him, and his response is first rage, then sadness, then a desire to reconnect.

In her 1945 paper 'Oedipal Complex', Klein outlines the difference between girls and boys, using her case studies with two

10-year-old children: Richard (see Chapter 6) and Rita (who was two-and-a-half years old when she began her analysis with Klein). The boy's Oedipal development, as with the girl, begins in the oral stage, according to Klein. The boy wants to possess his mother, but also to protect her insides from the father's contaminating penis. His rivalry and hatred is expressed in a desire to bite off his father's penis. This arouses his own fear that his father will retaliate and castrate him.

The concept of 'womb envy' was conceived by Karen Horney, Klein's contemporary in Berlin. Klein adopted this in her thinking, believing that little boys feel disadvantaged by their inability to have babies and feel inferior to the mother. This is a boy's 'Femininity Complex' (Klein, 1928), to which he responds with a 'narcissistic over-estimation of his penis'. When love for his mother and his internal objects predominate, his penis and faeces become reparative gifts, nurturing and creative. He begins to identify with the good father, enabling him to face his castration fear and establish security.

The female version of the Oedipal Complex begins in a similar vein but diverges in crucial points, according to Klein. She stated that vaginal masturbation is more frequent in childhood than most people care to admit. (She also controversially wrote in 1928 that masturbation is not as gratifying for girls as it is for boys, and that girls are more jealous creatures due to their penis envy). The girl is aware of the 'receptive nature' of her genitals: rather than a desire to have a penis, as in Freud, she desires to receive the penis. She has 'unconscious knowledge' that she contains potential babies, and is in competition with her mother, who has the breast and the father's penis as well as real babies.

Anxiety arises from a desire to rob her mother of her babies and the father's penis, which she fears will result in the mother robbing her own insides of unborn babies (just as the boy fears his father's retaliatory castration). While the boy's main anxiety object is the castrating father, the girl's is the persecutory, almost magical mother.

Girls, according to Klein, have a richer inner life of internalized objects, and a stronger drive to introject objects, which in turn creates a great dependence on the outer world and need for love. Thus, introjecting the good, loving mother is important to a girl's healthy development. The 'masculine position' is transformed from envy and a desire to possess her father (specifically the penis) via seduction, to an introjection of a creative and powerful, perhaps ambitious, part of the Ego, nurtured by her internal mother imago.

The Oedipal crisis will morph in the Depressive Position into one of separation and loss. Rather than loving and hating the split parent part-objects and envying the combined figure, the child now realizes that his parents are separate, whole objects. He has loved, hated, feared, and needed these objects, but now he also sees them as whole people in a relationship from which he is excluded.

On top of that, he is afraid of his own anger and destructiveness, afraid he will become unlovable. His wish to protect his parents from his own anger helps him find his own loving feelings in a healthy outcome. Klein suggested that a child begins to accept the parental relationship not just through fear, as Freud suggested, but also through love. The child wants the parents to love each other and, together, to love their baby.

The Positions in Adults

The Paranoid-Schizoid and Depressive positions are in a continual shifting balance throughout our everyday life. Someone or some situation may at any time ignite our anger or persecutory anxiety, which we may then work through with some of the painful realizations of the Depressive position.

In some people, particularly those diagnosed with Borderline Personality Disorder, Paranoid-Schizoid defences can become fixed and may then be used constantly in destructive behaviour patterns. Reality is not denied (as in schizophrenic patients), nor is it acknowledged and accepted (as in the Depressive position). Instead, perceptions are perverted and distorted, so that paranoias are confirmed and omnipotence is 'proven', as in the Paranoid-Schizoid defences. In her paper 'On Criminality' (1934), Klein wrote: 'It is not lack of conscience, but the overpowering strictness of the Superego, which is responsible for the characteristics of asocial and criminal persons.' For Anna Freud, it was the collapse of the Superego that led to asocial tendencies.

To move through the Depressive position is to become more integrated, but accepting the reality of loss and guilt is too much for some people to bear. They fear integration to the point where they may feel impossible to work with; they may even get some kind of perverse thrill in distorting the truth. In therapy, the therapist may be pulled into the counter-transference of fury and helplessness that is so powerful that the therapist may find it hard to pull back and resume an objective position.

For Kleinians, the aim of psychoanalysis is to enable the client to tolerate the Depressive position more securely – although it is never fixed, we all topple into paranoid phantasies and polarizing viewpoints. This echoes Freud's aim to help patients achieve a state of 'ordinary unhappiness'. Psychoanalyst Jaqueline Rose (1993) has noted that, especially in the USA, Klein's work has been rejected because of her violence and negativity. Klein herself wrote: 'My method presupposes that I have been from the beginning willing to attract to myself the negative as well as the positive transference.' Klein sits with the difficult emotions that her patients find hard to bear and helps them accept the complex, dark realities of relationships, the loss implicit in love, the annihilation implicit in life. When a therapist is able to tolerate these for a client, it dissipates their unbearable force. The question that continues to be asked by Klein's critics, though, is this: Whose reality was Klein interpreting – her clients' or her own?

6. Case Study of a Young Boy

In June 1940, Klein left London for the village of Pitlochry, Scotland, at the request of the parents of one of her patients. The family had moved up to Scotland and wanted Klein to continue her analysis of their 10-year-old son, Richard, which was to last four months. In the first month, she decided to keep extensive notes immediately after each session which she would continue to revise until her death in 1960, and which became her final book and gift to the psychoanalytical world, *Narrative of a Child Analysis* (1961). The book includes 74 drawings (some of which can be viewed on the melanie-klein-trust.org.uk website) and a detailed description of each of their 93 sessions. She acknowledges in the introduction the accuracy of note-taking but argues against doing it within the session as it interrupts the analytic frame. The name of the boy has been changed to Richard, and the location from Scotland to Wales. Klein calls herself Mrs K.

The Case Study Begins

Richard was 10 years old when Mrs K. began his analysis. He was very frightened of other children and preferred the company of adults, particularly women. He avoided going out by himself, was hypochondriacal (about himself and his mother) and subject to depression. Since the age of four or five, his increasing withdrawal and lack of interest in activities had been a cause of concern for his parents. The outbreak of war, in 1939, occurred when Richard was eight, and his symptoms became so acute at this point that he was unable to attend school. As a result of the war, his family moved temporarily from London to Scotland, and leaving his home town had further increased his anxieties. He was afraid of air raids and bombs, and he followed the news closely; his preoccupations came up in the analysis. It was a particularly tense time in the war – the continuous bombing of London, the invasions of Athens, Crete and Russia, and the sinking of the Bismark.

Richard was also in many ways a precocious and gifted child, Klein added in her introduction. He was musical, loved nature and words, and had a 'feeling for the dramatic which enlivened his conversation'.

Richard and his mother stayed in a hotel in Mrs K.'s village during the week, returning to their Scottish home at the weekend. Mrs K. was renting a playroom for child analysis at the time (she saw her adult patients in her own lodgings). This was a large space that was sometimes used by the Girl Guides, hence contained a number of books, toys and a large wall map of the world. As there was nobody to answer the door, Mrs K. collected the key; if Richard was early, he sometimes met her on the road and walked back with her after. Outside the 50-minute sessions, she states, she avoided interpretation and kept the conversation light. In the course of the 'treatment', Richard produced drawings, which Mrs K. kept and interpreted as 'gifts' even when he expressed a wish to take them home. Mrs K. provided play material, and the crayons and pencils he used to draw also represented people in his play. He brought his own set of toy ships.

Family Background

Richard was the youngest of two children; Mrs K. records that his brother was eight years older and had been sent away to school (in reality, the brother was 11 years older and had joined the army). Klein also notes that breast-feeding had been unsatisfactory and lasted a few weeks. He had always been a delicate child, and his mother reported two operations: circumcision at three years and tonsillectomy aged six.

His mother was inclined towards depression, highly anxious and worried about her son's health. Klein notes that Richard was a disappointment to her; she preferred the older brother who had been a success at school and never caused her any worry. She experienced Richard as very demanding: over-anxious, over-affectionate and clingy. His mother pampered him without having much confidence in him, yet was patient with his anxieties. His father was very fond of him but distant, and he had little in common with his older brother.

First Session

Mrs K. prepared a table with toys, a writing pad, pencils and chalks. Richard ignored the toys and looked at her, expectantly. She told him she knew he had some difficulties and wanted to be helped. At once, he began to talk about his worries. He was afraid of boys in the street and of going out. It made him hate school. He spoke about Hitler and was aware that Mrs K. was Austrian. He spoke about a bomb that fell near their old house and gave a 'dramatic description of what had happened' – a window had been broken and he was worried about Cook who was still there. He was also worried about what he was like inside and what other people's insides were like.

Mrs K. asked whether he was also worried about his mother. He said he often felt frightened, 'lonely and deserted' before going to sleep. He worried about Mummy's health. He also feared a tramp would come and kidnap Mummy in the night. He then imagined saving her by scalding the tramp with hot water and making him unconscious.

Mrs K. suggested the tramp may seem to him like Hitler. She then suggested Richard was worried that Daddy's genitals might injure Mummy at night. When Richard became frightened by her interpretation, she asked if he knew what genitals were. At first, he said no, but then said Mummy told him that babies grew inside her, that she had little eggs and Daddy put fluid inside her that made them grow. He went on to say Daddy was kind and wouldn't do anything bad to Mummy.

Mrs K. pointed out that when he thought of the tramp, he did not remember that Daddy was also in the bedroom and could protect Mummy. She suggested it was because Richard felt Daddy himself might hurt mummy. 'Richard looked impressed and evidently accepted the interpretation,' she wrote. Night-time Daddy could be hurting Mummy even though day-time Daddy was nice and kind. Klein noticed he seemed less tense than when he had arrived and was happy to come and talk to her the next day.

In her note following the first session, Klein wrote that she did not use the language of psychoanalytical interpretation with her young clients. She instead used their language and did not interpret the transference as Freud did with his adult patients. She also checked with the mother beforehand what words Richard used for genitals, urination or defecation, but was told he had none and never referred to them. 'In a case where repression, encouraged by the environment, has gone so far that no name for the genital or bodily function exist, the analyst has to introduce words for them.' Klein's gifts to Richard, then, were the words 'big job', 'little job', and gradually, later 'sexual relations' and 'faeces'.

Middle Sessions

In early sessions, Richard spent a lot of time exploring the hut, and was particularly interested in the map on the wall where he would discuss his concerns about the Nazi invasions. Slowly he began to play and brought his own toys, such as his battleships, which he would line up in harmony or crash together, or arrange in positions such as two battleships alongside one another.

Then he started drawing. His drawings were mostly of battleships, which he named, as well as starfish and fishes. He

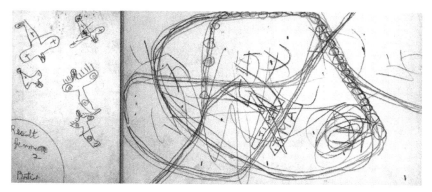

Fig. 6 Two drawings by 'Richard', 1941

spoke a lot about his worries about the war (he was very well informed and read the news), his concerns for his mother's health, his envy of his brother and his dog, Bobby. Meanwhile, Mrs K. would interpret his actions and thoughts. She interpreted exploring the room as exploring his mother's insides; the crashing of the boats was his parents having sexual intercourse; his destructive play and drawings were expressions of his Oedipal conflict and the surfacing of earlier Paranoid-Schizoid positions (the greedy devouring babies and punishing Superego 'combined parent figure'). His enjoyment of the garden or happy drawings, according to Mrs K. revealed his desire for reparation; his fascination with her clock as his fascination with her insides; and the old electric fire, which he kept turning off and on, represented his fear that in wanting to attack the bad things (unborn babies, his father's genitals) in his mother's insides might kill her, equally his greed for her 'inexhaustible and ever-present breast' (it is worth noting that Klein was writing her paper on Envy at the time). Everything is Oedipal, but in some cases – as Richard reminds her – a fish is just a fish.

Here is an example of session three:

> *[Richard] soon turned to the map and expressed his fears about the British battleships being blockaded in the Mediterranean if Gibraltar were taken by the Germans. They could not get through Suez. He also spoke of injured soldiers and showed some anxiety about their fate. He wondered how the British troops could be rescued from Greece. What would Hitler do to the Greeks; would he enslave them? Looking at the map, he said with concern*

that Portugal was a very small country compared with big Germany, and would be overcome by Hitler.

Mrs K. interpreted that he also worried unconsciously about what might happen to Daddy when he put his genital into Mummy. Daddy might not be able to get out of Mummy's inside and would be caught there, like the ships in the Mediterranean... He was also afraid that Mummy would be hurt by the Hitler tramp-Daddy. Thus he felt anxious about both parents and guilty because of his aggressive wishes against them. His dog Bobby stood for himself wanting to take his father's place with Mummy (the armchair standing for the bed) and whenever he felt jealous and angry, he hated and attacked Daddy in his thoughts. This also made him feel sorry and guilty [Oedipus situation].

Richard smiled agreement at Mrs K.'s saying that the dog stood for himself, but disagreed emphatically with the other part of the interpretation, because he would never *do* such a thing.*'* (Klein's emphasis)

In Session 12, Richard makes a drawing of a ship, the lower half under the water which he said 'had nothing to do with the upper part'. Underwater there was a hungry starfish which liked the plant. There was a fish swimming which he said was mummy, and the starfish was baby. He also drew a U-boat and a ship. In her case study, Klein notes that she interpreted these items as follows:

'...*the hungry starfish, the baby, was himself; the plant, mummy's breast which he wished to feed from. When he felt like a greedy baby, who wanted his mother all to himself and could not have her, he became angry and jealous and felt he attacked both parents. This was represented by the U-boat that 'probably' would attack the ship... He said everything that went on under the water had nothing to do with the upper part. This meant that greed, jealousy, and aggression were not known to one part of his mind, were kept unconscious. In the top half of the drawing, divided from the lower half, he expressed his wish to unite his parents and have them happily together. These feelings, of which he was quite aware, were experienced in what he felt to be the upper part of his mind... Richard had followed this interpretation with great interest and attention and clearly felt relief.'*

By Session 16, Klein notes that his drawings are fully expressing Oedipal conflicts. Her interpretations are essential to help him 'integrate the split-off and contrasting aspects of himself'. By session 22, he is more forthcoming in expressing his negative transference, his persecutory anxieties about Mrs K.'s loyalties in the war – is she a spy? In session 24, Richard makes a drawing of a starfish-empire with a red border: the starfish Klein interprets as Richard 'greedily internalizing the mother'. In her notes, she adds that

'...the red border represents the process of Projective Identification. The greedy part of himself – the starfish – had invaded the mother; and Richard's anxiety, feelings of guilt, and sympathy related to his mother's suffering both through his intrusion and through the

bad father damaging and controlling her internally. In my view the processes of internalization and Projective Identification are complimentary and operate from the beginning of post-natal life; they vitally determine object-relations.'

His fear of other children – including those who lurked around the streets of Pitlochry and called him 'Italian' – became linked in Mrs K.'s Oedipal interpretations to his fear of the unborn children in mummy's stomach, who he felt he attacked with his 'big job' (session 26). He was afraid that when he attacked the children, they would retaliate.

As Mrs K. throws a light on his negative, aggressive feelings towards his parents, Richard becomes more anxious, especially when his mother is ill. She notes that it is as though he thinks his feelings have made her unwell and this upsets him deeply. She writes in her notes to session 27:

'Such despair is an inherent part of depression and it is first experienced during the Depressive Position. Since early destructive impulses are felt to be omnipotent, they are in a sense felt to be irreparable. When they are revived at any stage of life, they retain some of the omnipotent character of infancy. Furthermore, the feeling that destructive impulses cannot be sufficiently controlled increases this revival of primal anxieties.'

As the sessions move on, Richard becomes more attached to 'the room' and Mrs K. and views their work as 'important' and good for him, although he's not exactly sure how. In this space, he is able to express his conflicts at home and his deepest fears, without Mrs K. growing ill like his mother, who thinks he talks too much. However, Richard does often worry that Mrs K. may die (and when she does, he asks, will she find him another analyst?). He is able to express his aggressive as well as positive feelings, good and bad, and she is able to tolerate and contain them; keeping his drawings, but also the room, the place, and providing consistency.

A Turning Point in the Therapy

Session 33 marks a pivotal point in Richard's therapy. Klein offered him a session on a Sunday (most sessions are Monday to Saturday) as he was too ill to go home for the weekend. He was happy and felt bolder about dealing with other boys. Mrs K. said it must be a relief to 'need not to pretend to be friendly while he was afraid of being attacked'. Richard 'strongly agrees'. Mrs K. observes his 'present feeling that he contained more of the good Mummy (and Mrs K.) – owing to the analysis which he found helpful – gave him greater security and made him better able to fight his internal as well as his external enemies'.

In this session, Richard also talks about his real circumcision and Mrs K. links this to his fears of Daddy attacking his penis, because when Richard is jealous of Daddy and Paul (his brother), he wished to attack their genitals. Richard listened with interest, she says, and asked if that was why he wanted to fight the other boys.

'In the last two days, Richard's mood had changed. He was less sad, manic defences and denial had diminished, and he felt more hope and trust. He was also more

*responsive to Mrs K.'s interpretations. A few days later,
Richard's mother came to see Mrs K. She reported on
Richard's progress; she had noticed a striking change
in him following this Sunday session. Although he was
very aggressive at home, he seemed much more friendly
and less tense and easier to get on with.'*

In following sessions, Richard's 'greater capacity to experience
and express his aggression' comes out in his disagreements
with Mrs K. In her notes, she observes that her continuing
interpretations – while distressing to him 'in particular those
relating to his mother's genitals' – clearly relieve his anxiety.
She states that while some doubt the ability of children to
understand such 'complicated interpretations' her experience
has shown her otherwise.

Of Mrs K.'s counter-transference during these analytic
sessions, Klein does not say a great deal. In one session near the
end, during which Richard is acting up destructively, Mrs K.
becomes 'impatient' with him, 'which, being unusual, frighten[s]
him very much'.

In session 36, Richard brings a cap with a broken peak which
Mrs K. interprets as symbolizing his 'damaged genital' after his
operation. 'Richard replied that he had thought, while he was
speaking to Mrs K., that she would explain it the way she did.'
Mrs K. asked if he thought the explanation was correct, to which
he replied 'Oh yes', then with embarrassment told her that last
night he was worried that his genital had been very red. She asked
what he thought about when he touched his genital, to which he
does not reply 'but did not deny that he had been masturbating'.

In session 39, Richard tells her he is no longer afraid of going out. 'Today a little girl had walked just behind him and he had also met a boy, and it did not matter at all. He was surprised at how little it mattered.' Halfway through the analysis, Klein told Richard of her plans to go to London to see her son, Erich, who had been called up to serve in the army. Richard was distressed about her departure and was afraid she would die (quite a reasonable fear at that time). He was also concerned he would be lonely without her.

On her return, Mrs K. found him withdrawn and Klein writes that the resistance had reached a climax, which she puts down to 'the analyst leaving him at a time when his feelings of loss and distrust were very strong'. She also notes that resistance comes up 'again and again' to certain interpretations but does not find this unusual. The process of 'working through', which Freud deemed so essential to analysis, she says, involves revisiting certain material (memories, dreams, events) many times, so that new details arise in the conscious mind each time, and allow a fuller analysis of the situation. This revisiting only occurs as defences or resistances repeatedly block acceptance of an interpretation and tends to occur around interpretations that are 'most painful, such as those of destructive impulses directed against the loved object'. Ultimately, however, this helps the Ego face and deal with split-off anxieties (both internal and external) and also split-off love, where this has not allowed itself to be felt because of its links to 'destructive impulses and persecutory anxieties' (Klein, 1961).

Klein notes over the next few sessions that Richard, no longer afraid of other children, has moved from the persecutory anxiety of the Paranoid-Schizoid position to the sadness of love, guilt and loss of the Depressive Position.

She noticed that since her return from London, he had been unable to look at her (except once). She told him that because he was so worried about his internal enemies (represented in one drawing as a monster daddy and 'horrid bird mummy'), including a fear of being poisoned or made ill by his bad desires, he had needed to keep his Mummy 'good', while Mrs K. had become very 'bad' (thereby splitting the mother into two mothers: one good and one bad).

Klein believed that by interpreting Richard's negative transference feelings towards her (as an expression of his 'primary aggressive feelings towards both parents and the resulting fears of having injured them irreparably') rather than ignoring them, she had found the only way to diminish his anxieties at the root, 'thus helping the patient to gain trust both in himself and his objects. Attempts to bring about a positive transference by neglecting the analysis of the negative one cannot, I believe, achieve lasting results'. Slowly, with 'fluctuations' in mood between manic and depressive defences, he became more reflective, took an interest in his drawings and material from previous sessions, and referred to 'the bad mummy'. He seemed happier when his fears about his internal enemies had been interpreted and understood.

> *'My experience has shown me that when guilt and depression can be borne to some extent and are not warded off by regression to the Paranoid–Schizoid position with its strong splitting processes, further steps towards Ego-integration and synthesis of objects occur'* she wrote in her notes to session 54. *'Together with this, hate is more mitigated with love.'*

The Final Sessions and Ending

As the ending approaches, Klein is watchful of her positive counter-transference, making sure she keeps her focus on analyzing Richard's anxieties and negative transference. When he says that she has 'lovely eyes', she notes that he sounds false and artificial; in fact, he swings between hostility and affection for her. Richard counts the days and becomes obsessed with the clock that had represented Mrs K. in earlier sessions. He has several violent outbursts, one in which Mrs K. has to restrain him, at one point becoming impatient with him 'which, being unusual, frightened him very much' (see above). Richard seems to have regressed to the Paranoid-Schizoid position, Klein notes, wishing to preserve and destroy her internally, enraged at her departure, and quite competitive with her. Adding to his anxiety is the fact that his father had become ill a month before. The 'combined parent figure', when internalized, becomes more virulent.

In session 87, Richard arranged the stools in the room into two lots: one side, he said, consisted of genitals of men they had talked about, including his Daddy's, his brother Paul's, Hitler's and Goering's – Hitler's being the biggest. On the other side was Richard's, Good Daddy's and Good Paul's. The stools went into battle, and his side was victorious: his play was aggressive and destructive. He said, 'poor playroom', meaning Mrs K. and mummy's insides. He began to interpret his drawings, telling Mrs K. what the figures represented. He also became sad and expressed a wish to be cuddled. Klein wrote in her notes that one of the features of the last sessions was his conscious and unconscious decision to finish the analysis in a friendly way, managing to control his aggression. 'He used the stronger belief in the good internal

Mrs K. and mother, and the good father, to ward off the fear of parting and his depression.' In her final notes, Klein mentions that Richard was depressed, and 'when so clinging, asked to be kissed'. She notes: 'Should not kiss him, parting.'

Klein's Conclusions

In her notes, written years after the ending, Klein feels that the diminution of Richard's persecutory anxieties was achieved by repeated interpretation of his internal objects and destructive impulses. 'The working through is made possible only by the analyst following these fluctuations closely and analyzing them.' Also, Richard's progress was bound with his improved relation to the good-object: his mother and Klein. She noted that idealization is linked with persecution, and it was only when Richard stopped idealizing his mother that trust and love could be established. Owing to the analysis of the Oedipal Complex, his love for his father could be more deeply experienced.

This was the significant conclusion that Klein drew from this case study: through witnessing Richard's struggle to integrate love and hate, it became clear that the Oedipus complex comes from the growing awareness and love from a child towards its parents, not from its hate and subsequent guilt. It coincided with the Depressive Position and had little to do with Freud's libidinal urges.

What Happened to Richard?

Klein's biographer Phyllis Grosskurth met 'Richard' when he was in his fifties, and described him as well-travelled, 'sociably alone', and completely unaware that he was the subject of a book. He remembered the analysis very well – 'it was very much a strong interest in genitalia' – and said that he had tried to see Klein again when he was 16 and in London, but she was 'frosty'. When he read the book, the smell of the ether in his circumcision and the sight of his fallen father, tea dribbling from his mouth, came back to him with force. He believes those two incidents affected him profoundly (Grosskurth, 1986). When Grosskurth handed him the book, he kissed the picture of Klein on the back cover and said: 'Dear Melanie'. His mother continued to correspond with Klein when Klein returned to London, as she was still concerned about Richard's aggressive behaviour, but Klein said she could not help, and slowly the mother began to accept Richard for who he was, not the 'normal' son she expected him to be.

Critiques of the Case Study

André Green (1927–2012) takes a critical view of the process of constant interpretation, saying that an analysis 'conducted solely through interpretations of the transference often puts the patient under unbearable pressure. The analysis takes on an aspect of persecution even if these interpretations are designed to help the patient understand what is happening within him' (Green, 1997).

John Padel (1913–99), an Independent in the British Psychoanalytical Society objected to the 'matriarchal world' the patient and analyst were locked into. The 'mother is never allowed to seem anything but the best, unless contaminated by father, Richard or his eldest brother'. This is interesting in light of Phyllis Grosskurth's assertion that Klein, in her diaries, never allowed her own mother to seem anything but the best. While unquestionably revisionist, even today this is nothing short of revolutionary: a mother who is not to blame for everyone's ills? In

Mothers: An Essay on Love and Cruelty (2018), psychoanalyst Jacqueline Rose argues that motherhood, in Western culture, is where we lodge the reality of our own conflicts. It is 'the ultimate scapegoat for our personal and political failings, for everything that is wrong with the world, which it becomes the task – unrealizable, of course – of mothers to repair'. You could say that Klein takes that Projective Identification and puts it back where it belongs, making it the responsibility of the individual to accept the reality of being fully human.

Hilary Clark, a Canadian researcher in psychoanalysis, cites Rose in her essay on Klein's case history: 'Complicating Disorder: The Play of Interpretation and Resistance in Melanie Klein's Narrative of a Child Analysis' (2011). Rose claimed that interpreting the boy's distress about the war and his own resettlement in Oedipal terms, Kleinian analysis 'makes of the analyst a fool and a fantast' (1993). Clark looks at the power-play between Richard and Mrs K., noticing how Klein reframes Richard's resistances to his interpretations in her narrative. As a bright child, Clark notes, Richard would know that seeming to 'play along' with Klein is an extremely effective defence. She writes: 'Klein is like Freud in that both tend to emphasize the authority and knowledge of the analyst as the one who interprets, not the one who is interpreted' which is a powerful way to restructure the dynamic in a more inter-subjective way. However, Klein saw the analyst as more of an expert, and her job with children was discerning the unconscious meanings of the child's symbolic play and then conveying these meanings to the child. Clark says that Klein 'worked on the assumption that, as long as they are addressed in simple, non-technical language, children can understand Oedipal interpretations of their play as doing things with breasts and penises'. For example, children can understand that bumping toy carriages together symbolizes parents 'bump[ing] their "thingummies"... together' (Klein, 1932). They can understand these things because they are sexual and aggressive beings, from birth, according to Klein (and slightly later, according to Freud). It was through 'deep' interpretations that Klein aimed to reduce the child's anxiety, Clark says, through exposing their most anxiety-provoking sadistic phantasies.

Clark notes that 'while Mrs. K. acknowledges and refers to Richard's fears of Hitler and German bombs, she sees his depression as arising not so much from the war as from the Oedipal anxieties that these conscious fears have "stirred up".' (1961) In every case, as psychiatrist R.D. Hinshelwood (b.1938) suggested in his 1994 book, Clinical Klein, 'the child's worries signify something else'. So Richard will overcome his fears, says Clark, 'only when his worries, questions, and dreams about the war and Hitler are interpreted in terms of the Oedipal war within'.

In November 2017, British child and adolescent psychotherapist Margaret Rustin delivered a paper titled 'Revisiting Melanie Klein's Narrative' to the Melanie Klein Trust and Royal College of Psychiatrists in Pitlochry, Scotland, where Klein had worked. In this paper Rustin acknowledges that when Kleinian students at the Tavistock Clinic, London, read the Narrative (which they do, apparently, day by day over four months), half are impressed by the analytical vigour, the other half shocked by the 'immediate plunge into analytic interpretation of the child's sexual phantasy and her readiness to address the negative transference'. She points to another element in the analysis which Klein herself does not explore: the relationship between the child and Mrs K. After session 33, where Klein agrees to see Richard after an illness, there is a positive change in Richard's attitude that his mother also notices. Rustin suggests the change partly occurs due to Klein's kindness: 'The generous quality of her concern for him is most evident, and one might suggest that his kinder attitude to himself is related to an internalization of this more benign figure.'

Kleinian analysts Hanna Segal and Donald Meltzer (1922–2004), both of whom were analyzed by Klein herself, have pointed out that the detail in the Narrative can seem overwhelming to the student, but most of the insights were a retrospective evaluation in light of her subsequent experiences. They draw attention to her technique: interpretation, mobilization of anxiety, increase of material, further interpretation, relief of anxiety. 'Melanie Klein,' they say, 'always believed that insight was the chief therapeutic agent in analysis and the main line of defence against repression after termination' (Grosskurth, 1986).

Reading this case study in today's climate, where nursery school teachers are not even allowed to touch a distressed or injured child, can be quite unnerving; particularly those points when an older woman is telling a young boy that he wishes to put his genital into her. Even in context, it may seem a bit extreme. Yet for this very reason it may be essential reading today, as it shines an interesting and uncomfortable light on our own confusion and fear around children and sex. Parents of young children may recognize their physical and visceral curiosity about their bodies and bodily functions, as well as a young child's obsession with their parents' stomachs, breasts and genitals. To see this manifest as anxious phantasy enacted through play begins to make sense. That Klein's (somewhat relentless) interpretations frighten or repulse the child doesn't mean that her ideas are frightening and repulsive, rather that we – and the child – have been brought up to view them that way. Most of us still can't bear the thought of our parents having sex, despite the fact it gave us life. Klein, in a way, normalizes and accepts the more painful phantasies – the aggression towards our parents, internal and external – by simply stating them as fact, by accepting them. This seems to assuage the guilt and its 'manic defence', which gives rise to so much anxiety and inner conflict in Richard. It also enables him to recognize his own courage and resources, to be curious, and to relate to objects internally and externally with increased awareness.

Conclusion: Kleinans Today

Melanie Klein was such a monumental figure in British Psychoanalysis, particularly child analysis, in the 1940s and 1950s, that it is astonishing how much she has been largely forgotten, not so much in the field of psychoanalysis itself (modern-day Kleinian analysts are very much at large across the UK), but certainly in the public consciousness. Her theories are, like Freud's, highly symbolic, metaphysical and visceral, and so perhaps in some way 'too much' to be popular. After World War II, the American School (which adopted the Ego psychology of Anna Freud) dominated psychoanalysis and continues to do so; the more creative innovators such as Klein and Jung seem to have fallen by the wayside. Yet their ideas are more commonplace than we perhaps acknowledge. The punitive Superego, the introjected persecutory object, is now more often referred to as the Critical Voice, or the Inner Critic. The concept of splitting has become central to trauma therapy, as patients with PTSD are understood as having split off their traumatized parts, so that they can continue to function in everyday life. During therapy, however, they may project these split-off parts into the therapist by the process of Projective Identification. It has been observed that Projective Identification also occurs in groups, which is why group behaviour tends to be primitive – one member finds they have a forcefully defined unconscious role to play for the whole group. Often, for instance, 'guilt' is projected into one person who then takes on the role of the scapegoat to assuage uncomfortable feelings in other members of the group.

A student trying to understand Klein's theories today may identify with Wilhelm Reich, who wrote: 'To read her is like being in a graveyard with open, putrefying bodies'. With good and bad breasts, two-year-old children full of hate, wanting to attack mothers' bellies full of faeces and penises, some of her 'planetariums' (Laing) of the infant mind seem like horrific mobiles of body parts dangling over the crib. Some of the blunt directness of her language may stem from the fact that she only learned English in her forties, when she migrated to England. Psychoanalyst Donald Winnicott would soften the mother–child relationship considerably (Kleinians view his ideas as sentimental; Adam Phillips calls them simplistic, 'a wry version of pastoral'), but it was Klein who dared to contradict Freud, to shine a light on the importance of the mother, as opposed to the father, in the development of the Ego. John Bowlby would later go on to explore this interaction – the mother–child relationship – in detail in his extremely influential Attachment Theory.

Modern Kleinian Analysis

There is an old joke that a patient arrives late for his analysis with Melanie Klein. She greets him saying, 'You're late! You've already missed two of my interpretations!' While it's true that Kleinian analysis continues to place huge value on interpretation, Modern Kleinian psychoanalysis has evolved to a gentler, more recognizable form in practice, particularly with adults. The setting is familiar to most modern forms of therapy, with two chairs facing each other in a room, unencumbered by desks or notes. The relationship is key, and the therapist listens with empathy as well as being aware of and using the transference and counter-transference relationship, introjection and projection, and Projective Identification. Although there may be a lot less interpretation than Klein herself used, the Kleinian frameworks of the positions and object relations continue to provide the map of unconscious and developmental processes.

According to Kleinian Psychoanalyst Margot Waddell, 'Klein's theory of developmental positions provides a good framework for dealing with states like narcissism, and envy, both of which can be very difficult in relationships' (quoted by Derrington, 2012). Envy can be very important: some people always begrudge other people their happiness; many of us would rather console a friend who has suffered a catastrophe than congratulate one who has had a success. This shift between a self-centred view of the world, in which we see things in black and white, and a more sophisticated view where we can see shades of grey and other people's points of view is a fundamental part of Klein's theory of development. Wadell notes that these views are known as the Paranoid-Schizoid position and the Depressive position respectively. The names have nothing to do with mental illness – they are simply the Kleinian terms for these ways of thinking about the world.

Robert Wasker, a San Francisco based couples' psychoanalyst who developed Modern Kleinian Therapy, says that the Kleinian technique can be used anywhere between one and five times a week.

He cautions however that infrequent visits cause more difficult transference and counter-transference situations and higher levels of Projective Identification. This is a robust way of reaching patients for whom he says, 'change or growth is experienced as a danger to self and object'. Wasker explores loss as a feature of the Paranoid-Schizoid position as well as the Depressive, creating a reliance on extreme Projective Identification and Splitting in adults. 'Klein suggested envy was often a factor in Projective Identification, representing the forced entry into another person in order to destroy that person's best qualities.' (Wasker, 2002).

Lavinia Gomez, who traces the lineage from Klein to Bowlby in her book An Introduction to Object Relations (1997) describes a modern object relations therapy in practice. She notes how projective defences are used by an anxious patient who brings his stress about the journey to therapy 'because of the baby's absolute need for another to be a part of his intense emotions'. He may force onto the counsellor 'his internal malignancy' or project a 'powerful saviour'. 'The splitting characteristic of this stage means the projections are extreme and unrealistic.' In this situation, perfectly competent counsellors find themselves giving extra time, disclosing too much or worrying about the client between sessions. Therapists should always question whether their counter-transference feelings are their own or the client's, but also need to be aware of the 'subtly different flavour' of Projective Identification.

For Gomez, 'concepts such as projection, splitting, denial, repression, transference and the relational framework help [therapists] to focus in detail on relational processes. So too do Klein's concepts of the Paranoid-Schizoid and Depressive

Positions'. She adds that there is an immense courage to Klein's work in shining a light on the most difficult and darkest aspects of being human, which her theory helps us to bear through scrutiny, rather than positivity. On the other hand, at its core is a reliance on the good object and 'expresses her commitment to the primacy of relationship. The core of the self is the confluence with another, underscoring our inescapably social nature' (Gomez, 1997).

Indeed, one could say that Klein's astute here-and-now observations of her child clients (much like US psychoanalyst Daniel Stern detailing the minutiae of mother–baby interaction) has provided therapists with a new way of paying close attention to the subtle but vital communications, conscious and unconscious, of clients. This close attention, which may have arisen from Klein's acute sense of the loneliness at the core of the human condition, is the essence of the Kleinian therapeutic relationship.

Klein's last, posthumously published paper was called 'On the Sense of Loneliness' (1997). She writes,

> *'However gratifying it is in later life to express thoughts and feelings to a congenial person, there remains an unsatisfied longing for an understanding without words – ultimately for the earliest relationship with the mother. This longing contributes to the sense of loneliness and derives from the depressive feeling of an irretrievable loss.'* (Klein, 1997)

Bibliography

Works by Klein

Klein, M. (1928) 'Early stages of the Oedipus conflict', *The International Journal of Psychoanalysis*, Vol. 9, pp.167–180

Klein, M. (1932) *The Psycho-Analysis of Children*, London: Vintage (this edn 1997)

Klein, M. (1935) 'A Contribution to the Psychogenesis of Manic-depressive States', *The International Journal of Psychoanalysis*, Vol. 16, pp.145–174

Klein, M. (1936) 'Weaning' in M. Klein (Ed.), *Love, Guilt and Reparation and Other Works 1921–1945*, London: H. Karnac (Books) Ltd.

Klein, M. (1945) 'Mourning and its Relation to Manic-Depressive States', *The International Journal of Psychoanalysis*, Vol. 21 pp.125–53

Klein, M. (1948) A Contribution to The Theory of Anxiety and Guilt', *The International Journal of Psychoanalysis*, Vol. 29 pp.114–123.

Klein, M. (1963) 'On the Sense of Loneliness' in M. Klein (Ed.), *Our Adult World and Other Essays*, New York: Basic Books, Inc.

Klein, M. (1992) 'Early stages of the Oedipus conflict (1928)' in *Love, Guilt and Reparation and Other Works 1921–1945*, London: H. Karnac (Books) Ltd.

Klein, M. (1997) *Envy and Gratitude and Other Works 1946–1963*. London: Vintage

Klein, M. (1998) *Love, Guilt and Reparation and Other Works 1921–1945*, London: Vintage

Klein, M. (1961) *Narrative of a Child Analysis: The Conduct of the Psycho-analysis of Children as Seen in the Treatment of a Ten Year Old Boy,* London: Vintage (this edn 2012)

Other works cited

Breuer, F. and Freud, S. (1893) 'On the Psychical Mechanism of Hysterical Phenomena: Preliminary Communications', *The Standard Edition of the Complete Psychological Works of Sigmund Freud, Vol. II* (1893–1895), Hogarth Press (1957)

Carpy, Denis V. (1989) 'Tolerating the Countertransference: A Mutative Process', *International Journal of Psycho-Analysis,* Issue. 70, p287

Clark, Hilary (2011) 'Complicating Disorder: The Play of Interpretation and Resistance in Melanie Klein's Narrative of a Child Analysis', *Atlantis: Critical Studies in Gender, Culture & Social Justice,* Vol. 35, Issue 2, p30

Danto, Elizabeth Ann (2007) *Freud's Free Clinics: Psychoanalysis & Social Justice 1918-1938,* Columbia University Press

Derrington, Andrew (2012) 'Kleinian Psychotherapy'. Available at: http://www.derrington.org/journalism/psychotherapy/kleinian-psychotherapy [Accessed 12 April 2019]

Freud, S. (1909) 'Analysis of a Phobia in a Five-Year-Old Boy', *The Standard Edition of the Complete Psychological Works of Sigmund Freud, Volume X (1909): Two Case Histories ('Little Hans' and the 'Rat Man'),* Hogarth Press (1953–74)

Freud, S. (1915) 'Instincts and Their Vicissitudes', *The Standard Edition of the Complete Psychological Works of Sigmund Freud, Vol. II (1893–1895),* Hogarth Press (1957)

Freud, S. (1952) *On Dreams,* Hogarth Press

Gomez, Lavinia (1997) *An Introduction to Object Relations,* London: Free Association Books

Greatrex, Toni S. (2002) 'Projective Identification: How Does it Work?' *Neuropsychoanalysis: An Interdisciplinary Journal for Psychoanalysis and the Neurosciences*, Vol. 4, Issue 2 pp.183–193

Grosskurth, Phyllis (1987) *Melanie Klein: Her World and Her Work*, New York: Alfred A. Knopf, Inc.

Heimann, Paula (1952) *Developments in Psychoanalysis*, London: Hogarth Press

Hinshelwood, R.D. (1994) *Clinical Klein: From Theory to Practice*, London: Free Association Books

Hinshelwood, R.D. and Robinson, Susan (2014) *Introducing Melanie Klein: A Graphic Guide*, London: Icon Books

Holmes, H. (1992) *The Inner World Outside*, New York: Routledge

Kendrick, W. and Meisel, P. (Eds) (1986) *Bloomsbury/Freud: The Letters of James and Alix Strachey 1924–1925*. New York: Basic Books

King, P. and Steiner, R. (eds) (1992) *The Freud/Klein Controversies 1941–45*, London: Routledge

Melanie-klein-trust.org.uk (2019) *Melanie Klein Trust* [online] Available at: http://www.melanie-klein-trust.org.uk/ [Accessed 15 Feb. 2019]

Miller, Jonathan (1983) *States of Mind*, New York: Methuin

Mitchell, J. (Ed) (1986) *The Selected Papers of Melanie Klein*, London: Penguin

Ogden, Thomas H (1979) 'On Projective Identification', *International Journal of Psycho-Analysis*, Issue. 60, pp.357–373

Pfeiffer, E. (Ed) (1985) *Sigmund Freud and Lou Andreas-Salomé: Letters*, London: Norton

Phillips, A. (2010) *Winnicott*, London: Penguin

Psychoanalysis.org.uk (2019) *Institute of Psychoanalysis*, [online] Available at: http://psychoanalysis.org.uk/ [Accessed 10 Jan. 2019]

Rose, J. (1993) *Why War: Psychoanalysis, Politics, and the Return to Melanie Klein*, Oxford: Blackwell

Rose, J. (2018) *Mothers: An Essay on Love and Cruelty*, London: Faber and Faber

Rosenfeld, H (1971) 'A Clinical Approach to the Psychoanalytic Theory of the Life and Death Instincts: An Investigation into the Aggressive Aspects of Narcissism', *The international Journal of Psycho-analysis*, Issue 52, pp.169–178

Rustin, M.E. and Rustin, M.J. (2016) *Reading Klein*, London: Routledge

Rustin, M.J. (2017) 'Revisiting Melanie Klein's Narrative of a Child Analysis: some thoughts about contemporary approaches to clinical practice in the light of Klein's fearless approach to interpretation', *Melanie Klein Trust* [online] Available at: http://www.melanie-klein-trust.org.uk/ [Accessed Apr 3 2019]

Schreiber, Mathias (2012) 'The Age of Excess: Berlin in the Golden Twenties', *Spiegel Online – International*. [online] Available at: http://www.spiegel.de/international/germany/spiegel-series-on-berlin-history-the-golden-twenties-a-866383.html [Accessed 5 Apr. 2019]

Segal, J.(1985) *Phantasy in Everyday Life*, London: Penguin

Segal, H. (1989) *Klein*, London: Karnac

Shwartz, A. (2008) *Shifting Voices: Feminist Thought and Women's Writing in Fin-de-Siècle Austria and Hungary*, McGill-Queen's University Press

Van der Kolk, B. (2014) *The Body Keeps the Score*, New York: Viking

Vickers, J. (2008) *Lou Von Salomé: A Biography of the Woman who inspired Freud, Nietzsche and Rilke*, North Carolina: McFarland and Co.

Waddell, M. (2002) *Inside Lives: Psychoanalysis and the Growth of the Personality*, London: Routledge

Wasker, R. (2002) *Primitive Experiences of Loss: Working with the Paranoid-Schizoid Patient*, London and New York: Routledge

Wittenberg, I. (1970) *Psycho-Analytical Insight and Relationships (A Kleinian Approach)*, London: Routledge

Zaslavsky, Jacó and Manuel J. Pires dos Santos (2005) 'Countertransference in Psychotherapy and Psychiatry Today', *Revista de Psiquiatria do Rio Grande do Sul*, Vol. 27, pp.293–301

Biography

Lucy Etherington is a published writer and journalist with a BA in English and Drama from Goldsmith's University, and a BSc in Integrative Psychotherapeutic Counselling. She lives in Suffolk with her family and continues to research and write alongside running a private clinical practice as a psychotherapist.

Acknowledgements

I'd like to thank my talented editors Sarah Tomley and Alice Bowden for their guidance, clarity, hard work and good humour – much appreciated when writing a book on Klein. I am also grateful to my family for their encouragement and for tolerating the chaos of books on the kitchen table.

Picture Credits:

Fig.1 Melanie Klein, aged 7–8, c. 1890. Albumen print by Atelier Olga, Vienna. Wellcome Library, London. **Fig.2** Melanie Klein, 1899, aged 17. Albumen print by Carl Pietzner. Wellcome Library, London. **Fig.3** Melanie Klein with her grand-daughter Diana, c.1994. Wellcome Library, London. **Fig.4** Ernest Jones, Melanie Klein and Anna Freud (date unknown). Wellcome Library, London. **Fig.5** Toys used by Melanie Klein. Wellcome Library, London. **Fig.6** Two drawings by 'Richard', 1941. The Wellcome Collection, London. All pictures used from The Wellcome Library, London are licensed under the Creative Commons Attribution 4.0 International licence.

Who the hell is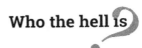

This exciting new series of books sets out to explore the life and theories of the world's leading intellectuals in a clear and understandable way. The series currently includes the following subject areas:

Art History | Psychology | Philosophy | Sociology | Politics

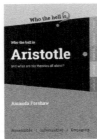   

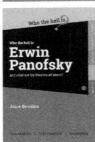 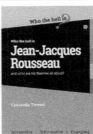  

For more information about forthcoming titles in the Who the hell is...? series, go to: **www.whothehellis.co.uk**.

If any of our readers would like to put in a request for a particular intellectual to be included in our series, then please contact us at **info@whothehellis.co.uk**.